CAN SELL....
WILL SELL

CAN SELL....
WILL SELL

A Step by step guide to successful selling for sales people and small business

We show you how to:

Be an effective face to face and social networker

Make effective telephone sales calls

Conduct productive meetings

Make powerful PowerPoint presentations

Successfully negotiate and close the deal

MIKE WHITE

www.cansellwillsell.com

On-line sales training, coaching and management support

authorHOUSE®

AuthorHouse™ UK
1663 Liberty Drive
Bloomington, IN 47403 USA
www.authorhouse.co.uk
Phone: 0800.197.4150

Published by AuthorHouse 01/12/2015

ISBN: 978-1-4969-9978-8 (sc)
ISBN: 978-1-4969-9980-1 (hc)
ISBN: 978-1-4969-9981-8 (e)

Library of Congress Control Number: 2014922817

Acknowledgements and thanks

I am truly thankful for the support of family, friends and acquaintances that have been with me during the highs and lows that come within a life in sales.

Several of these have specific experience in business that has helped me turn an idea into a reality and I would like to thank these in particular.

Philip Waite (www.threetiermedia.com) for his continued wise counsel in business and for his generous assistance and contribution to **www.CanSellWillSell.com**

Ian Crocker (www.absolutelearning.co.uk) for sharing his life experience in coaching and training throughout the years.

Martyn Willis for being a client turned close friend with a mutual interest in advertising sales management over too many years to remember. His personal support has been invaluable.

I would also like to thank contributors for their input into **CanSellWillSell:**

Special thanks to **Alan Donegan** (www.enjoypresenting.co.uk) for his excellent content on effective use of PowerPoint presentations. Alan trains companies like Microsoft, Pepsi and Air Arabia on how to present, communicate and have more presence -it always makes him smile that he runs PowerPoint workshops for Microsoft. He is an award winning presenter, radio show host and occasional entertainer!

Mark Hughes (www.smallbitemarketing.com) for sharing his valuable knowledge on social media.

Also thanks to **Andy Szebeni** (a true networking exponent now trainee teacher) for his contribution to the networking and customer service sections of this book

Others deserve a mention for supporting me in bringing **CanSellWillSell** together:

Bob King (www.bkanda.co.uk) for using his vast experience as a business coach in giving a great perspective and sanity check on my approach to the sales process.

David Saunderson (previous business partner and now communications advisor for Macmillan Cancer Support) for his patience and dedication during the early stages of development of this book.

Nick Lambrou for using his skilled attention to detail in checking content and style prior to publishing.

The knowledge, ideas, techniques and approaches that I have developed and shared with you have come from numerous sources and I would like to acknowledge those unknown to me for their wise council over the years

Preface

In today's increasingly competitive world, your approach to making sales within your working week has a major effect not just on generating new business but also on client retention and growing your sales by keeping ahead of your competitors.

Networking, telephone contact, face to face meetings and social media are all important in developing sales. How you integrate these activities into your sales strategy is a key ingredient to success in finding and retaining clients. Ultimately people buy from people and you will need to talk to prospects to gain their trust. Emails and on-line contact alone just won't do!

Put bluntly, you may be working in the best business in your market, but that means nothing if you don't provide communicate with prospects to let them know what you do. **CanSellWillSell** helps you avoid being a best kept secret!

This book will give you the confidence, skills and knowledge to build strong business relationships with new and existing clients through effective selling.

Here is a practical step by step guide to the simple 10 stage sales process, which will allow you to feel confident in taking full control of your sales calls.

Key learning areas will include how to

- Network effectively-face to face and on-line
- Make powerful presentations
- Negotiate and close deals

Each chapter clearly identifies the learning you will enjoy and finishes with your own check list, so that you can refer to key areas of learning easily and quickly,

> We also highlight a number of '**MUST DO's**" throughout the book which are also brought together within the book summary. If you do nothing else, by doing these simple 'must do's' you will already have a more effective approach to successful selling.

Ready?-Let's get started!

As a sales person or small business owner or partner you are already using some good sales practices-but do you know it?

In everyday life we are undertaking sales activities.

- Making a call to a customer to ensure they are satisfied with your product or service-that's selling.
- Following up on an enquiry from a website-that's selling.
- Calling people to ensure they have received your literature-that's selling.
- Inviting someone to connect with you on LinkedIn-that's selling

....and attending a networking event-that's definitely a great sales opportunity!

You all ready selling-you just need a structure to work with to maximise results.

The pathway to successful selling is based on <u>ten</u> simple steps which we take you through during this book broken down into four easy to read chapters.

The Ten Steps to Successful Selling

We hope you enjoy this introduction to sales. **CanSellWillSell** could be the most profitable book you ever read!

Chapter 1

How to plan and prepare
for successful selling

Step i) Planning and preparation

To ensure long-term prospects and profitability, it makes sense to develop a broad base of customers, rather than relying on a few. The most effective marketing activities (e.g. website enquiries, mail shots, PR, social networking) are those supported with consistent follow up telephone calls followed, where appropriate, by effective face to face meetings.

To start with then, a telephone sales campaign is the beginning of the sales process (often supporting your marketing activities) leading to profitable new customer relationships being developed.

Objectives and Scope

In this chapter we will show you how to:

- Devise and implement a telesales plan which will open the door to a meeting and increase your customer base
- Feel confident and enjoy contacting prospective customers on the telephone and face to face
- Keep accurate and useful client records

You will be able to:

1. Feel more confident and positive when calling prospects
2. Plan an effective telesales strategy
3. Understand the basic principles of executing the plan

You – The Salesperson-never!

Before we start, here's some good news!

To make effective sales calls, you don't have to be a sales hotshot! You are good at what you do and probably have got some experience in selling. As we said in the preface, there is a basic structure you should work to no matter how experienced you are:

- Preparation-mental and physical
- Powerful Introduction in under a minute
- Fact find-engaging with the client
- Confirming needs-gaining agreement
- Presentation-effective meetings and use of PowerPoint
- Recommendation=geared to customer needs
- Close-overcoming objections and getting agreement to buy

Just getting your preparation and a powerful introduction under your belt will help you fly! Why?

Because the first steps will bring success by having the right mental approach:

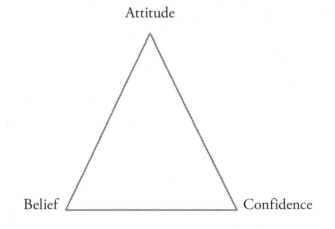

Planning an Effective Telesales Strategy

It's all down to planning, '*fail to prepare - prepare to fail*' is a well worn truism and is as relevant now as it has ever been. Take time to think carefully what you want to achieve and how you are going to realise this.

Key considerations:

- Objectives
- Target Market
- Research
- Time management

Objectives

Remember, your objective might not be to make a sale over the telephone right there and then, but rather to open the channels of communication so you can start to develop the relationship with the prospective customer that will end in them buying from you.

Just finding out more about the prospect's needs or getting an appointment from your telephone call could be a great result!

When setting your goals, follow the SMART principle; in other words, keep your objectives:

Specific
Measurable
Achievable
Realistic
Time Framed

An example of how to set up a SMART objective follows:

EXAMPLES OF SMART OBJECTIVES

Specific   I will make telephone calls
                I will aim to speak to decision makers

	I will get appointments
Measurable	30 telephone calls
	5 decision makers
	1 appointment
Achievable	You might not know if your objective is achievable first time round so you will need to review this as you go along. You want to try to stretch yourself.
Realistic	As for Achievable
Time framed	The specific objectives will be completed in 3 hours on (date)

A complete SMART objective might be:

I will make 30 telephone calls to try to reach 5 decision makers and make one appointment. I will make the calls between 10.30 am and 4.30 pm on Tuesday (date).

After the session, you would then review whether the objective was realistic and achievable and adjust (up or down) as required. It might also prompt you to consider what you could do differently to increase your performance and target.

Target Markets

The key to success is to understand what prospective customers you wish to approach and what you are offering them that they will want. Think in terms of how what you will be offering will overcome their problems or the obstacles they face; put yourself in their shoes.

For example you might be providing them with:

- A service, which will improve efficiency resulting in saving time and frustration
- A product that will reduce costs
- Expertise leading to improved levels of service to their customers

Getting their need and why your offer is important to them clear in your mind will ensure you define a strong introduction to your call. The call introduction is covered later in this guide.

The following chart shows clearly the sectors/categories you should prioritise to maximise the effectiveness of your *new business* call plan:

For your first sales approaches, there are clear benefits to defining your prospects by category in this way. By prioritising categories/customers within which you have expertise, (1st priority in the diagram above) you will generate more impact in your sales call. It doesn't matter if this experience is through a limited number of customer relationships, it's perception that counts, as you will be able to:

- Demonstrate an understanding of what they need
- Use testimonials from similar customers – name-dropping is a powerful tool
- Be able to use a referral from an existing customer - this is very powerful! (Make sure you ask for referrals from your customers whenever possible)

You now have an outline plan that has *measurable objectives* aimed at a *specific target market* and we can now move on to executing the plan.

Getting Your Prospect List in Place

Another key to preparation is having a prospect list in place. This should include name, company telephone number and a comments section. This will be invaluable in getting good momentum – see later. The simple approach is to make an excel spreadsheet:

A	B	C	D
Company Name	Decision Maker	Phone Number	Comments/Next action

As you develop customer relationships, it will be important to do two things:

1. Keep email correspondence and attachments in files; and
2. Keep details of calls and diary reminders for follow ups

At this stage, it might be worth moving from an excel spreadsheet combined with your diary to using a database or as it is often known; a customer relationship management (CRM) system.

This is covered in more detail in this chapter.

Building Your Customer Prospect List

How do you get customer names to put into your spreadsheet or database?

There are various ways of doing this. The best are those which you generate yourself from immediate contact or referrals from existing customers (DON'T FORGET TO ASK!).

Don't forget the power of Networking-we cover this in Chapter two:

- Face to Face Networking: Collect as many business cards as possible and become an effective networker.

- Social Networking: Make sure you are using your networks (e.g.LinkedIn, Facebook) as prospecting tools

Other approaches include:

- Affiliates: Use your contacts to agree an approach to the same people with different/complementary products
- Prize draws: Offering a prize to your visitors and guests is a great way to generate contacts. Retailers – you can devise a simple quiz or questionnaire
- Referrals – Get full details from customers
- Become a member of associations (Chambers, industry) – this provides invaluable access to databases

You can also use other approaches, which are also useful, but which may generate data that isn't completely up to date or complete:

- Media (press) - adverts and editorial
- Internet searches/websites for extra details
- Local papers
- Directories
- The local library
- Online Media (e.g. Yell.com)
- Trade directories

You now have an outline plan that has *measurable objectives* aimed at a *specific target market* and you have *identified a list of people to call.*

Understanding the Basic Principles of Executing the Plan

'All men are the same-it is their habits that set them far apart.'

Confucius 551-479 BC

The key to ensuring the plan is well executed is to develop positive habits, which will avoid unnecessary blocks to the new business initiative.

In addition, by making customer prospecting a habitual part of your working week, you will become increasingly confident, be more effective and gain momentum, which will lead to the generation of new customers.

You will also make your own luck and will find that opportunities will arise from unexpected sources. Remember, Gary Player (one of the most successful international golf players of all time) once famously said:

'The more I practice, the luckier I get.'

Research

Within the planning and preparation stage, it will be useful to do some basic research on the company you are calling. This will instil greater confidence when talking to the customer and make them feel valued and are genuinely interested in helping them:

- What is the decision maker's name? Note it on your spreadsheet of contacts.
- The customer's web site (for businesses) might give you some clues as to where you may be able to help them specifically.
- Does the customer use one of your competitors? Try to find out beforehand if you can.
- Do I know my competitors' offering and am I clear on the advantages I have over them?

Time Management

As a small business, there are a number of distractions that can prevent a strong new sales plan from getting underway.

Sometimes, these are real and important priorities (e.g. customer meeting, product development) and occasionally, they are manufactured and imagined (filing, tea break)!

Try these simple tips on a regular basis. They will develop positive habits.

TOP TIPS

1. Set aside specific, bite size times a week for new business calling. Try to block off the same time/days every week, ideally using 10am-1pm and 2.30pm-4.30pm as key times. These tend to be the best times to approach customers.
2. Avoid distractions:
- Turn off email and mobile phone (Try to make calls on a land line)
- Don't let other activities distract you
- Allocate specific regular break times
3. Have your list of prospects, with contact details; in front of you (excel spreadsheet). Make sure there is a section for comments to make a note of action points before going on to the next call. This will mean that you are able to maximise upon the number of calls made during the time available.
4. Ensure that you take appropriate and timely action from the calls you have made.

To summarise so far: To get yourself ready for your sales calls:

- Set yourself realistic goals
- Prioritise customers within sectors that you have knowledge of/ contacts in. Include referrals within these
- Have relevant testimonials to hand to use during the call
- Build your list of prospects to call
- Research these prospects
- Develop positive habits:
  - Plan good quality time each week for sales activity –and keep to it!
  - Have your list of prospects in front of you and make appropriate notes
  - Take appropriate and timely follow up action

OK, you're nearly ready to go for it!!

Powerful Introduction

The final part of the planning stage is to ensure there is a powerful introduction to your sales call. Getting the first 60 seconds of the call sorted out in your mind is crucial in terms of building your confidence and engaging the customer. It is also important as it sets the scene and tone for the rest of the call.

The key to success is the ability to say what your business does concisely and how its goods or services can benefit the prospect (by solving a problem).

Here's a process to do this:

Write down what your company offers rather that what it does. Customers want to know from you what is in it for them. They *buy results, not services or products.*

Practice this, so that it flows from your mouth in under 30 seconds.

You now have the basis for the 60-second introduction to the call:

1. **Confirm you are talking to the correct person (15 seconds).**
2. **Relay your 30-second speech. Practise on family, friends or colleagues to see how it is received – or use a recording device and then listen to yourself.**
3. **State what the product/service is achieving for similar customers (use testimonials if appropriate).**
4. **Ask a question that gets the customer talking!! By this, we mean a question to which they can't simply answer "yes" or "no" (see below).**

Closed question: Are you interested?

Open question: Tell me more about.......... (Your company/service/need)

Confident and Positive Sales Calls

You are now ready to go and you've got your ABC of sales under your belt!

Attitude

- You've done your preparation and you are set to pick up the phone
- The key now is to be positive, believe in yourself...and have fun!
- Sounds tricky? It doesn't have to be

Belief

- Don't forget, you have an expertise which is of real value to prospective customers.
- You are so good; you owe it to your prospects to sell to them!
- Don't worry if it isn't right for some of the people you contact - just move on to the next prospect on the list! At least by making contact and finding out, you no longer wonder whether they might be a customer.
- Remember **SWSWSWSW** - Some will, some won't, so what!... someone's waiting.

Practice

The more you do, the more comfortable you will feel and rejection will become less of an issue in your mind. If they don't buy in to what you have to say, maybe it isn't right for them at this time. After all, you don't buy something every time you walk in to a shop. Plus-remember golfer Gary Player: *The more you practice (i.e. do those calls), the luckier you will get.*

What is rejection anyway?

- Treat it as feedback.
- Thank the person and take any learning from it that you can.
- It is a single number. The next call could be the successful one!
- It isn't personal, it's an action.
- The prospect is rejecting your proposition - not you!
- You are no worse off having made the call – at least you know more than when you started.

Confident and Fun Sales Sessions

You will feel confident and enjoy making calls more if you make the most of your SMART objectives.

Making the objectives achievable will mean that you can come away from calls feeling a winner!

Examples of achievable targets:

- I will feel more comfortable discussing my company on the phone
- I will make 25 calls and get through to 5 decision makers
- I will find out what 3 customers need
- I will make two appointments today

Finally, put in place measures of success. Celebrate these when they occur!

Put your objectives on a white board or other prominent place and record every time you are a winner.

Agree with yourself rewards for success and set aside regular breaks to celebrate!

Conclusion

Remember - You are good at what you do!

Speak to as many potential customers, using the tools and tips in this guide and you *will* win new customers.

- Plan an effective telesales strategy with SMART objectives aimed at customers within sectors you have expertise
- Develop positive habits in executing the plan. Research, prepare and then make the calls. This approach will make you feel more confident and positive when calling prospects
- Implement a 'contract to yourself' to help keep you on track. Review performance and adjust, as required, on a regular basis

Checklist - Your Contract with Yourself

The following checklist summarises the key points of this guide.

We recommend that you complete and review it on a regular basis and use it as a live document.

I will spend (   ) hours a week contacting prospective customers

I will set aside   Monday   Tuesday   Wednesday   Thursday   Friday

Preparation	Yes/No
Time allocated	
Distractions minimised. Mobile and email off	
Research done	
Prospect list in place	
60 second intro in place	
Measurement and rewards in place	

Devise SMART objectives

- **S**pecific
- **M**easurable

- **A**chievable
- **R**ealistic
- **T**ime framed

Remember. *You are good at what you do for customers.*

Prioritise approaching customers in the same sectors that you currently have expertise in and use existing customers for referrals and testimonials.

My top customers are:

Customer	Sector

Step ii) Lead generation

The power of Networking

Before we get into the sales process, let's take a look at networking. Earlier, we suggested several ways of developing your contacts and database, with networking top of the list.

This takes two forms-face to face networking and on-line social networking.

Why network? We know that a really powerful way to increase the number of customers we have is through referrals. Networking (face to face and on-line) allows you to meet potential clients and referrers on a regular basis, which builds their understanding and confidence in what you deliver. They get to like you and trust you!

From there, do an exceptional job for a customer and they will recommend you to others and return themselves. It's an upward spiral.

Another good reason is that it can be a fun way of meeting and/or interacting with people and making acquaintances and friends who can give you advice and support when you need it.

Don't get carried away though! Whilst this is an excellent way to increase the size of a customer database, it is not a good idea to rely solely on this method. Plan your networking activity on a weekly basis to fit into your schedule. Once a day is a target to aim for, including breakfast, lunch, evening events and on –line social media.

Networking is a powerful way of ensuring you are constantly in potential customers' minds and in sight of other businesses that might refer others to you. But what is effective networking? What is the appropriate way to network? We've all heard of 'push' and 'pull' marketing. It's a good idea to avoid 'push' networking and adopt a 'pull' networking strategy instead.

Objectives and Scope

In this chapter we show you how to

- Be confident when attending network meetings
- Develop effective business relationships through networking
- Use the power of Linkedin and social media to generate a sales pipeline

After reading this you will be able to:

- Understand the approaches to different types of networking groups
- Prepare for confident and effective networking events
- Maximise business opportunities from social networking
- Develop meaningful relationships following the meeting

The power of Networking-Face to face Networking

The 10 Golden Rules

There are several networking formats, each of which requires a specific approach. We come to this later. However, there are some basic tips for you to remember that are relevant to all types of network meeting events:

1. **Try to relax and go into the session to have fun- be yourself**
   - Take a deep breath and exhale slowly before you go in-this will slow your heartbeat and reduce nerves
   - Remind yourself of how well your last event went and how you are as good as everyone else in the room. They will be nervous too!

2. **Set yourself some realistic, achievable goals for the evening**
   - e.g. I will meet x number of potential important contacts
   - Speak to identified contacts (if given a delegate list at the beginning of the meeting)
   - Circulate for two hours and get x number of appropriate business cards

3. **Be approachable**
   - Smile, have good eye contact, ask questions about the person/people around you and listen –show interest
   - Take their business card and make a couple of notes as you talk-this demonstrates interest and will help you remember the discussion afterwards, so you can follow up

4. **Be prepared**
   - Have plenty of business cards and give these to people you have had a good chat with
   - Don't automatically use them like confetti, but take/create opportunities as they arrive

5. **Have a powerful, succinct answer to the question' what is it that you do'**
   - We go into some detail about this later, but make sure your statement tells them what you can do for them. Base your

statement on a benefit you provide to your customers, not a long statement of who you are and what you do

6. **Be memorable!**
    *   Appropriate humour works well with people. Finding a common interest can add as a memory jogger when you make contact after the event

7. **Move on**
    *   If a discussion has gone well, it is likely to only have been an introductory 'meeting of minds'
    *   When it is time to move on, thank the person for their time, take that all important business card and suggest that you will call them in a few days' time

TOP TIP: With the contacts business card in hand ask them if you can become a contact on LinkedIn. With their agreement you can send them a successful invite (as an email address is needed to do so) and know it will be accepted

After the event

8. **Making good contacts and collecting business cards, means nothing if you don't follow up.**
    *   Put details on your CRM system or database as soon as possible.
    *   Diarise a follow up call within a few days of the event to progress discussions
    *   Send an invite on LinkedIn and send an initial message of thanks for meeting you and remind them of your discussion

9. **Don't worry too much if you didn't achieve all of your objectives.**
    *   Learn from the experience and readjust your approach and/ or targets next time

10. **Decide whether the profile of the attendees is appropriate for you.**
    *   If not, try another networking group;-there are plenty to choose from!

Types of Networking Events

In this guide, we focus on three key types of networking groups.

- Formal
- Casual
- Speed networking

Formal Networking Events

These take place constantly and are a great way of letting people know who you are, what your company does and how you can help their business. The formal event is usually over a breakfast, lunch or early evening session.

This can be more comfortable than some less formal events because people know what to look forward to. It is expected that you will talk about your company and what you do. It is accepted that you will ask others about their company and what they do and therefore invite them to answer those questions.

Let's start from how to approach a formal networking event. As we've said. It is expected that you will be there to let others know about your area of work. If you can access the attendee list beforehand, try to do some research before the day. Accessing websites of the companies you might want to target prior to arrival will provide some information to enable you to open a meaningful discussion. Research individuals who are attending through organisations like LinkedIn, Plaxo, Ecademy and many of the other online networking sites that have sprung up recently.

These are incredible sources of information to use. Many business people place information about themselves and their companies on these sites, as well as previous employment and personal information. This could really help find something common between you e.g. did you go to the same school or university, do you enjoy the same activities, do you have mutual acquaintances etc? These are great ways of opening conversations with people. Links in constructing a bond with people quickly and establishing rapport is a good way to start to build the relationship.

Tip 1: Find something personal between you and the other individual and you'll break the ice quicker, as you'll have a positive thing to discuss straightaway, something you both enjoy and about which you will be animated.

Upon arrival at the event, you will most likely be handed your badge.

Tip 2: Always wear your badge on your right lapel. When shaking hands with someone, you automatically lean forward with the right side of your body; so, if you wear your badge on your left side, you are obscuring it. If it's on the right side, then it is prominent to the other person's view.

When you see a group of people engaged in conversation and the group dynamics are closed (no obvious physical gap for you to join them) then don't try to join that group. Move on to others and then come back once the group has broken up if there is someone specific you want to talk to.

Tip 3: No one likes to stand on their own at networking events so if there is someone on their own, that is the person to target. They will thank you for coming over and you'll be welcomed with open arms.

Opening a conversation, even at a formal networking event, with a 20-minute sermon about what you do is going to be counter-productive. Adopt the 80/20 rule. Talk for 20% and listen for the remaining 80%. Hopefully, the other person will have the same mentality and you'll end up with an even conversation. Use the 20% as a way of asking questions because people love talking about themselves. If you can get them to talk about themselves, they are feeding you great information about who they are, what they are looking for etc. You can then use this information in targeting your conversation.

> **Tip 4: Always say the person's name back to them in the first sentence three times; it helps cement their name into your head. We have all been in the situation where we've greeted someone and then forgotten their name and then someone else joins and asks us to introduce the other person. Focus on their face and say their name, audibly, three times in that first sentence. This will help you remember them the next time you meet.**

Pass the 'So What 'Test!

Now they've asked you what you do, do you tell them you're an accountant? If so, you're missing an opportunity to 'sell' to them without them even realising it. Focus on the benefits of what you do right from the first line. So:

> 'I'm an accountant' *becomes* 'I take away the fear and uncertainly of dealing with the tax man'

> 'I'm a conveyancer' *becomes* 'I relieve you of the anxiety of moving house by ensuring everything is in place for your move day'

> What you're doing here is focusing on the benefits of working with you, not the processes.

People don't care that you've been in business for centuries, they don't care that you've got lovely offices, they will be thinking WIIFM – 'What's In It for me'. What am I going to get out of this exchange and if you can hit them with exactly what they will get, right at the beginning of the conversation, you will capture their attention and keep it.

How and When to Move On

Moving on from talking to someone at a formal networking event can be tricky. Many people find themselves embarrassed about leaving someone and taking up a conversation with another person.

Tip 5: Everyone knows why they are there. They are there to talk to more than just one person so no one will mind you saying 'Thanks for the chat, I'm just going to chat to a few other people'. Don't 'make up' someone to move to so you can get away; this can seriously backfire if it's obvious you've made the person up.

When moving on, simply be honest with the person. If you feel there is something more you can both talk about, ask permission to contact them after the event on LinkedIn and by phone and exchange cards. Remember if you exchange cards with someone, you are giving them permission to contact you and they should not be ignored.

It is a good practice to follow up the event with an email to the person thanking them for chatting with you and, if appropriate, arranging a time for a further conversation or meeting. Invite them to another networking event you're attending so you can maintain the relationship and always speak to them when you meet at future events, even if it's just to say 'Hi'.

Casual networking

It can be more difficult to know how to work a room in a more casual networking event. This is where our focus should be on 'pull' rather than 'push' networking. For our purposes here, we define "push" and "pull" as follows:

- Push: Where you tell people generally what you do and how it solves their problems. This is generally used for groups or where there is little time to spend with someone that you have to get your elevator pitch in.
- Pull: Where you ask people about themselves so you can identify their needs and then tailor what you say, so that they are encouraged to come to their own decision as to how you might help them. This is generally used 1-to-1 where you have more time to explore.

In some ways, informal networking events can be more intimidating than formal networking groups. When registering upon arrival, you may find yourself entering in to a room full of people chatting away and wondering where to start!

The first thing to do is to remember the golden rules at the beginning of this guide and prepare yourself mentally.

As you enter the room, don't see the people as one big group. Survey the room and you will see that there are individuals on their own, small groups of 2 to3 people and much larger groups.

Where to Start?

Here are some practical tips to get you talking to people quickly:

Look out for people you know and get underway with them - they will soon introduce you to others. If this contact is already a close associate, as he/she moves on, try to separate and use the contacts they have introduced to you as your next networking. You can always agree to meet up later and compare notes.

Single people: They won't know anyone and will appreciate you breaking the ice.

Small open groups: Ones where body language and stance shows people are open to welcome new entrants. Look out for groups:

- In a horseshoe shape or (with a group of three) a loose triangle - not in a tight format, looking inwards
- Not involved in intense discussion, but where you can hear general chat.
- Where there seem to be several discussions going on. You'll be surprised as to how a seemingly large group can actually be made up of sub divided members
- With anyone looking around outside the group, with a welcoming smile/relaxed posture. Gain eye contact and make the approach with a brief introduction and extended hand to encourage a handshake

Put simply-look for groups where you can see welcoming faces, not hunched backs!

Don't Make Things Difficult for Yourself

Leave closed groups alone! They are happy as they are at present. If there is someone you particularly want to see, wait for a more opportune moment.

Don't enter larger groups unless you know someone within it: If this is the situation, walk up to your contact and say 'hello'-he/she will quickly get you involved with the group if you ask!

What Should I Say?

At the formal networking event, it is acceptable to tell people what you do, it's okay to 'push' your message out to the group but at casual networking events, it tends to be better to chat to people, get to know each other and just develop relationships. Allow people time to get to know you personally, about your personal likes and dislikes. You can still use the method of researching companies and people before you go but then focus on the person standing in front of you and don't look at them just as a 'company' or 'potential customer'.

Try to move the conversation away from business and on to a more personal level as this relaxes them and they feel more able to just chat. Remember that you do this day-in-day-out when you meet people grabbing a coffee in the kitchen, waiting on the platform, standing in line or on the train. Casual networking is really no different from these situations.

If you are able to find something unusual about you, or better still them, focus on that e.g. "My wife and I have just completed a tour of Italy for our 30th Anniversary." Use this style of information to really engage people and they are then more likely to remember you.

Or

At one event I met Chris and, as usual, I moved the conversation away from business because he told me that he'd just come back from holiday.

23

I immediately thought this is an opportunity to build rapport and get to know 'the person'. We then started talking about his safari and mountaineering holiday, both of which I had done and still do, and spent 25 minutes chatting about that.

People will buy from you because they like you 'and' you have a service or product they want. However, if you have a service or product they want 'and' they don't like you, they will not buy from you. How many times have you come out of a restaurant, having received rude service from the staff and said "I'm never going back there!' despite the food being good.

> Chris and I got on very well and after 25 minutes he said to me, "I suppose I should ask you what you do." When I told him he immediately said, "You must come into my company and do some work with us." The 25 minutes spent with Chris just chatting, getting to know him and developing a relationship resulted in two lots of work with his company.

Focus on the person in front of you and listen carefully for things that will enable you to get to know the person. It is very likely that conversation around work will follow but you're not 'pushing' your message out, you're 'pulling' the person in to like you and they are then much more likely to buy your product or service.

Just as in formal networking, the way to move on is the same. Thanking the person for the chat and saying you're going to chat to a few others. Before you go, ask if you can swap cards and if you do, then you are giving each other permission to make contact after the event.

> **Tip 6: When you meet someone at a casual networking event and you've spent time getting to know them, it's not a good idea to then go back to the office and simply add them to your database and send out 'blank' marketing messages.**

I received one recently where I'd been at a casual networking event and had a really good chat with someone who then sent me a message four days later saying "Dear Stewart, it was good to meet you last night or we may have chatted recently on the phone". What does that tell you about this person?

This is not the time to 'push' your message out but the time to 'pull' people into you as a person and not a company.

Speed Networking

This is another type of networking altogether and one, if done properly, can be enjoyable.

The room is set up so you sit facing another delegate and you have a fixed length of time to 'make your pitch'. This is the time where you really sell your services to another person. You can incorporate or deliver your elevator pitch and then answer questions the other person puts to you. Generally a facilitator will ring a bell after the prescribed length of time and you swap, so the other person has an opportunity to do their pitch. Once you've both spoken one of you then moves on to another person in the room and you start the process again.

Speed networking is a great way of 'pushing' your message to a large number of people in a short space of time. Now, what is the message you need to push?

Listen to them first if you can – it means you have more information about them when you come to speak and so can angle your benefits accordingly.

Your USP-The Value Proposition

Remember the WIIFM above? What's In It for Me? That is what the person will be thinking whilst your talking to them so you need to answer that question almost as soon as you start talking. Focus heavily, and honestly, on the benefits you and your organisation will bring to the other person at the outset of your pitch. Forget, at this stage, the processes and 'how' you achieve what you achieve. They won't be interested in the fact that you've been around for many years or the incredible accounts system you have, and they are unlikely to be interested in your location with the technology that's available today.

How can you make them more profitable, more efficient and pay out less by working with them? My elevator pitch (or speed networking pitch) is just sixteen words.

> You enhance your service, increase your profit and reduce your costs through my coaching and presentations.

This definitely passes the 'So what? 'test!

So as soon as I start talking, I am focusing on three benefits 'they' will enjoy when working with me. I then put in a couple of processes at the end. As soon as they hear better service, more money, less costs; they are interested in finding out how you achieve that. I could say:

"I am a business and schools coach; I do presentations and am an author"

So What?

… that doesn't tell them how they are going to have a better, leaner, more profit-generating company by talking to me.

Focus entirely on the 'benefits' your organisation will bring to theirs in a speed-networking situation.

> **Tip 7: Building rapport very quickly will move your relationship into a closer zone with the other person and help to move towards a 'working' relationship much quicker. Matching and mirroring body language is a great way to build rapport with people. It must be done with subtlety, with a great deal of integrity and should never be abused.**

Once you've established that there might be something for you to chat about further then exchange cards and see each other after the session or at a further meeting.

> **Tip 8: When you're listening to the person, try to think not only about how you can help each other but who else might you be able to put them in touch with for them to work together. This is a great way of building rapport, helping another business is likely to result in referrals back to you.**

If you offer to send any of the contacts at a speed-networking event something afterwards, make sure you do so. You will be seen as unreliable if you promise to do something and then fail to do so.

Following Up After the Event

Having swapped business cards and agreed with your contacts that you will be following up with a call and an invite to engage on LinkedIn

- Be sure to make that call and send that LinkedIn invite within the following week, so the initial contact is fresh in their mind
- Be positive. Remember, they are expecting your contact. Remind them of this
- Plan for the call. Do some research about the company
- Have your diary ready. Assume you are going to discuss opportunities now or make an appointment!

The power of Networking- Social Networking

We have mentioned above that your face to face networking activity gives you a great chance to develop your on-line contacts and have focussed ion LinkedIn. Although you can apply this to other social networks (e.g., Facebook), LinkedIn is by far the most effective way of establishing contact and rapport within the *business* community. Although not within the scope of this book, you can co-ordinate your activities within LinkIn, Facebook and Twitter and other social media to your website to improve profile and encourage response.

Questions you should be asking yourself

- Why am I inviting another person to connect
- What is your objective for connecting
- Potential client
- Mentor
- New business partnership
- Find a referrer

Reasons to send a LinkedIn invite or message:

1. You are asking one of your contacts for an introduction to someone in their network.
2. You are writing to someone you don't know, but you have a common connection or group.
3. Someone shared an interesting link that you read and you want to connect with them.
4. You shared an article in a group and someone read it, liked it and/ or commented
5. You sent an invite to connect and they have accepted so you want to thank them.

Types of desired results you expect when you send the message:

A key result to aim for is to begin the sales process we guide you through within this book.

This can mean:

- Subscriber acquisition (the start of the lead generation process)
- Securing a phone or in-person conversation (the start the sales process).

However there are other useful potential outcomes:
  - Referral/introduction to a new connection (grow personal network)
  - Idea exchange (promotes the possibility of a collaborative joint venture)

How to engage effectively with potential and existing contacts on LinkedIn

To guide you through here is a template for success

General Template Outline

1. Subject Line
2. Greeting
3. Confirm your commonality
4. Give reason why you are connecting
5. Always provide value
6. Call to Action
7. Close

Template #1: You are asking a group member for an introduction to someone in their network

Hi <Name>,

We are both members of the <group name>

I'd like to connect with <Name of the connection> in your network. I've been trying to make contact with <the connection's company> for a few weeks so If you know <Name of connection> well enough, can you introduce me?

At the same time if you need any help or an introduction please let me know.

Thank you for your help,
<Your Name>

EXAMPLE:

Hi Paul,

We are both members of the "Top 500 Entrepreneurs" LinkedIn group

I wanted to connect with Mary Riggs in your network. I've been trying to make contact with Usendo Ltd for a few weeks so If you know Mary well enough, can you please introduce me?

At the same time if you need any help or an introduction please let me know.

Thank you for your help
Mike

Template #2: You are writing someone you don't know, but you have a common connection.

Dear <Name>,

We are both members of the same LinkedIn group called <Group name>. I'm interested in learning from others who share the same challenges as me.

The advice and articles you have shared in the group are very interesting and if possible, I would like to connect with so I can follow your regular updates.

Best Regards,
<Your Name>

EXAMPLE:

Dear Paul,

We are both members of the same LinkedIn group called "Top 500 Entrepreneurs." I'm interested in learning from others who share the same challenges as me.

The advice and articles you have shared in the group are very interesting and if possible, I would like to connect with you so I can follow your regular updates.

Best Regards,

Regards,
Mike

Template #3: Someone shared an interesting link that you read and you want to connect with them.

Hi <Name>,

Our common connection, <Name>, re-posted an article you shared on <Day/Date>. I enjoyed the article, especially the part about <Enter 1 or 2 insights>.

I would like to read more of what you share as part of my LinkedIn network.

Regards,
<Your Name>

EXAMPLE:

Dear Paul,

Our common group member, Mary Riggs, liked, commented re-posted an article you shared yesterday. The article was an excellent read. Thank you for sharing.

I definitely agree with the author's main point that personal introductions work best in LinkedIn.

I'd like to read more of your posts as part of my personal LinkedIn network.

Best Regards,
Mike

Template #4: You shared an article in your network and someone read it.

Hello <Name>,

As we are members of the group <group name>, I wanted to reach out and say thanks for sharing my link today in the <discussion thread name>. Glad you felt it was worth forwarding on.

I'd be delighted to have you in my professional LinkedIn network so do let me know if you would like to connect and I'll send you an invite

Many thanks

Kind Regards,
<Your Name>

EXAMPLE:

Hello Jim,

As we are both members of the group <Advantage Strategies>, I wanted to reach out and say thanks for sharing my link today in the "How to identify collaborative opportunities" discussion thread.

Really glad you felt it was worth forwarding on.

I'd be delighted to have you in my professional LinkedIn network, so do let me know if you would like to connect and I'll send you an invite

Many thanks

Kind Regards,
Mike

Template #5: Someone you sent an invite to connect with has accepted and connected. You can use this follow up message.

Hi <Add New Connection Name>,

Many thanks for accepting my request to connect.

How are things going for you so far in 2014? Working on anything special?

If there is anything I can do to help you out or your network, please do reach out and let me know.

To get to know me a little better and what I do, I'd like to offer you a complimentary gift from (your company). It's a guide to 'How to Network effectively'

Click the link below to pick that up:

<Insert Link Here>

Thanks again for connecting and I look forward to chatting with you more soon.

Best Regards
< Your Name Here>

EXAMPLE:

Hi Jim

Many thanks for accepting my request to connect.

How are things going for you so far in 2014? Working on anything special?

If there is anything I can do to help you out or your network, please do reach out and let me know.

To get to know me a little better and what I do, I'd like to offer you a complimentary gift from **CanSellWillSell**. It's a guide to 'How to Network effectively'

Click the link below to pick that up:

www.cansellwillsell.com

Thanks again for connecting and I look forward to chatting with you more soon.

Best Regards
Mike

Linked In Formula for Success

1) To maximise the results you get from your networking you need to be easily found by fellow members and impress them when they get to your page.

You can achieve this by fully optimising and SPEAKING to your target audience:

Here are some Do's and Dont's:

    i)   **Do** use key words people would use to search for your type of business
    ii)   **Don't** set up like a c.v. It isn't about you-it's about how you can help them.
    iii)   **Do** have a professional image: have an engaging Biography headline-what do you do-how do you help?
    iv)   **Do** have an Informative benefit driven profile summary, based on your powerful Introduction we discussed earlier

You should also ensure that:
    i)   All your profile sections are complete
    ii)   You have a unique URL (eg.https://linkedin.com/in/cansellwillsell)
    iii)   Current activity, past experience, skills etc

2) Grow your network

Although you should aim for 500+ contacts, don't worry if you are not there yet. It is most important to nurture and gain the trust of the contacts you have by providing regular valuable information and then request to connect with their contacts you feel are relevant to you.

TOP TIP: You can only connect with people you know-but remember and harness the power of 2nd and 3rd connections.

Start with:

- Connecting with people you network with
- Importing your existing email data base (see the next section re databases)
- Connecting with members of a group-we cover how to join a group below

Remember Linkin is a referral network-Leverage its true power!

3) Prospecting

Offline and online new business opportunities will not just fall into your lap. You need to actively pursue your ideal target prospects.

The best way of doing this is via groups

When joining groups-join groups where potential customers are not where your competitors are active

How to join a group

To become a member of an open group (i.e. not one where you need to be accepted).

Go to the members tab

Add key words and geo modifiers into the search bar at the top right of the members page

Example: If you sell to the pub trade join the Gastro Pubs, Restaurants and Hotel/Managers UK Group.

Narrow down members and sent them a private message-this is not a pitch! Contact and engage-add value, provide advice, information and add value to gain trust

4) Nurture

The true value of LinkedIn is in the relationships you build over time. The more value you give to a relationship the more you will get back. You can use the message templates above to achieve this

Conclusion

Whether formal, casual or speed networking-or online, one fact is true of all networking - be honest, be open, be willing to talk to and communicate with anyone, you never know what might come of it. Be ready to give just as much and more than you get, it will come back to you at some point.

Be happy to refer to others in your network. Today's good deed may come back to you in some way tomorrow.

Above all, remember why you are at an event or engaging on-line…it's because you want to be!

Prepare well, be positive, approach as many people as possible in an engaging way and enjoy the occasion….. You will be successful.

Your Networking Checklist

MUST DO:

i)   To start: Make sure you have prepared youself well mentally and physically.Just before you enter the room, check in the mirror, remind yourself of a great thing you have done recently and enter the room chest out, shoulders back, exuding confidence!

ii)   To end: Make sure you swop business cards and ask to be engaged on LinkedIn-follow up soon afterwards with an invite

Review the first 7 of the10 Golden Rules of Face to Face Networking

- Try to relax and go into the session to have fun-be yourself
- Set yourself some realistic, achievable goals for the evening
- Be approachable
- Be prepared
- Have a powerful, succinct answer to the question' what is it that you do'
- Be memorable!
- Be memorable!
- Move on

After the event

- Making good contacts and collecting business cards, means nothing if you don't follow up.
- Don't worry too much if you didn't achieve all of your objectives.
- Decide whether the profile of the attendees is appropriate for you.

Formal Networking

- Can you get the attendee list? If so research and find common areas.
- Badge on right lapel
- Pick a group to join or individual to talk to
- Repeat someone's name to embed it in your mind
- At the appropriate time deliver your benefit statement that explains what you do
- Agree to follow up if appropriate
- Move on

Casual Networking

- Pick a group to join or individual to talk to
- Use conversational techniques
- Build rapport

- Agree to follow up if appropriate
- Move on

Speed Networking

- Have your USP pitch clear in your mind
- Try to listen first
- Adapt and deliver your USP pitch

Social Networking

- Make sure your profile is professional and up to date
- Join appropriate groups
- Share information and contacts feely-don't sell!

Remember always follow up!

Step ii) Keeping useful client records -continued

How to create a database

Using the various methods you have learnt about getting contacts, it i now important to organise your records. The last thing you really want to do is spend time looking for details that should be to hand.

Spreadsheets and card systems are fine up to a point, but a CRM (Customer Relationship Management) system is a database which helps develop, manage, and grow a business by retaining customers and building upon the customer base.

It saves you time and thereby money and is the foundation for action:

In this chapter, we show you how to implement an effective sales and marketing plan using CRM as a solid platform from which to start. This will lead to more profitable business from an increased customer base and effective use of your time, giving more precious hours to deliver to your customers!

Scope

After reading this section, you will be able to:

1. Consider the options for creating a database
2. Choose between database packages
3. Use the database in your business, specifically for planning your telephone sales call sessions

First Things First - Why Have a CRM System?

Simply put, a CRM system, used properly, will give you:

- Improved customer service
- Improved sales performance
- Increased sales and marketing effectiveness
- More time to focus on customer delivery

Within this, there are lots of reasons why businesses of all sizes rely on a CRM platform:

- Storing essential customer contact/relationship information in one place for easy access. Records stored in one place that can be updated and visible by authorised personnel
- Schedule marketing, sales and customer service activity and pipelines. Sophisticated systems can also implement planned actions, such as sending emails, letters about offers, products and services. They can also track responses and actions
- Integrate with accounts packages for more advanced analysis and customer order tracking
- Help work more efficiently by organising essential data. This can include calendars, task lists, priorities and alarms or reminders of when things should be done
- Enable searches of the database (especially if you have a large number of contacts) to find people by name, type, area, etc. In fact, data can be interrogated by whatever type of tags (or keywords) you want

By storing information, actions and follow up, businesses can analyse the effectiveness of sales and marketing campaigns as well as customer trends.

> **A solid CRM system is therefore a "must-have" in today's business environment! A CRM will store important customer/ prospect information, help you communicate effectively and treat people as individuals so you can establish and maintain long term and profitable relationships.**

Consider the Options for Creating a Database

Knowing about customers and potential customers and keeping track of them is vital to all businesses. The more you know about them the better you can meet their needs, now and in the future.

Options for a database and advantages/disadvantages:

Database Method	Advantages	Disadvantages
Bits of paper	Easy access.	Lacks detail, easily lost.

Notebook	Good detail.	Info not filed, easily lost.
Post-its	Easy access.	No detail easily lost.
Business card file	Accessible filing, inexpensive.	Cards can be misfiled, lost or damaged.
Spreadsheet	Easy to access Good for sorting detail by field.	Only basic client information shown. Not easy to build in reminders.
Off the shelf CRM	Relatively low cost, good level of client data, easily accessible and updated. Variety of marketing facilities (e.g. email, text)	More costly than manual systems. Some functions you need from CRM may not be available.
Customised CRM	Functions mainly relevant to your needs.	Cost v Benefit for a SME.
Purpose Built CRM	Totally relevant to your needs.	Cost v benefit for a SME.

There is no tangible benefit in keeping information on bits of paper and in notebooks. You can't access information easily, records may be lost and frustration will reign! As your notebook gets bigger it gets more difficult to find the record you want.

Business card files are fine for having quick access to telephone numbers and addresses when making calls, but this approach still relies on you accurately recording other information somewhere else, so you know what action to take after making the call. In all manual systems, actions get recorded more than once and information does not readily stand out for action to be taken.

So - in reality, you *must* have a database approach of some sort to manage customers.

The two key approaches for consideration are either to use your own spreadsheet or an off the shelf CRM that you can bespoke to your needs without too much work and cost.

Starting From Scratch

To start capturing clients' details, you may decide to start off with a spreadsheet. This approach will limit the ability to manage your diary for scheduling appointments effectively, record follow up actions and keep your records in one place. You will probably need an effective reminder and action system to work alongside, such as Microsoft Outlook.

If you do decide to start your records with a spreadsheet you should:

- Format the information in such a way that it can easily be imported to a CRM at a later stage when the client contact list is significant sized and there is a need to record more details
- Have a comments column so that client contact notes can be recorded for action

The following basic fields should be considered as a minimum are:

- Surname
- First Name
- Job title/role
- Company Name
- Address (Field 1)
- Address (Field 2)
- County
- Postcode
- Tel No.
- Mobile
- Fax
- Email
- Website
- Comments
- Type of Business
- Source (How you know the prospect)

Important Point – Future Proof

Make sure you always put information in the fields that is consistent across all records. For example if Address (Field 1) is the road name, it must always be the road name in each record. So in this example you might need an additional field if there is an address line before the road name.

How to transfer all of the information you have in various forms onto your new database.

The obvious way, is to simply type the information you have gathered on to the database, transfer in from a spreadsheet template, export from your email programme (e.g. Outlook/Outlook Express or the like). In addition, you can scan your business cards using a portable card scanner.

Choose Between Database Packages

For this next section, you've either decided to buy a CRM package from the outset or you have reached the stage where you now need to use a CRM database package.

When making your decision, you should consider exactly what different CRM programmes offer and their relevance to your business and what you want to use it for, remembering that the starting point of a CRM is to allow you to understand and respond to (or even anticipate) customers' needs. You might revisit the reasons why businesses use CRMs that we covered in the introduction earlier.

Start by making a list of objectives and the benefits you want to achieve. It might be that you will have to compromise on your requirements (perhaps to stay within an overall budget) so when you list out your requirements, afford each one a priority 1 (imperative), 2 (really want) or 3 (would be nice). That way, you will identify with ease those that meet your real needs.

These objectives could include some or all of the following:

- Increase the number of customers you have
- Get more business from existing customers
- Reduce levels of lost customers (attrition)
- Improve time management-doing several functions from one central point
  - Quotes
  - Invoices
  - Project Management
  - Email campaigns

- o Text messages
- o Improved filing of information stored in one place and easily accessible

The secret to an effective CRM package is not just what data is collected but also in its organising, interpretation and proactive use. Computers and databases can't transform the relationship you have with the customer alone. However, the effective use of a good computer based CRM solution will increase your understanding of customers' needs and heighten the chances of significantly increasing sales by developing relevant products and services and marketing them.

Software resellers are often good first line advisers as they have experience and feedback from selling competing CRM packages. Most of the big CRM software manufacturers have extensive advice, pdfs and guides on their sites that reputedly hold your hand through the selection process. They are likely to be biased, of course, but can be good sources of ideas. There are also independent CRM consultants who can provide good advice. Ask them first about how they earn their fees (by charging you for their independent advice or by commission on product sales).

An internet search for 'CRM systems for small businesses' will allow you to read reviews of many CRM systems and to evaluate services relevant to your needs, including pay-as-you-use options, hosted systems (i.e. where the data is actually held elsewhere and you access it via the internet) and those that are installed on your own computer system or PC.

Here are two examples of how a CRM application can work well for small businesses.

Improved Sales and Marketing

Building up your knowledge of customers' purchases and enquiries from you (date of purchase, product/service bought, quantity) is a powerful sales and marketing tool. By putting this information onto your CRM system you will be able to ascertain the buying preferences and habits of customers and allow you to send out tailored marketing material, promoting products and services. This will increase your chance of moving the sale forward. You can also use this information as the basis of your sales and marketing activity to similar companies within a particular sector.

Improved Customer Service and Sales Performance

A Good CRM system will flag inactive customers for you to contact. It alerts contract renewal dates so you can remind the customer in advance. This will increase your chance of retaining the client and allow you to sell additional, relevant products for a win/win result.

It is also possible to build a more personal relationship by noting details of the client (e.g. birthdays, family details, holidays, etc) so that an appropriate level of rapport can be built into conversations and /or appropriate marketing activity undertaken (e.g. birthday card).

You should be shown how to use these tools in the training your CRM provider gives you.

When looking at CRM solutions, you want to check the features and functionality

As part of any CRM research, make sure appropriate training is provided. Be sure to understand how this is done in your particular system. It could be anything from personal onsite training through to webinars at times of the day that you can't make (perhaps based on the time of day in another country). Using a CRM is easy once you know how, but the key is good training at the outset!

When you've narrowed the field down, ask each supplier to provide a full cost (including any modifications required), time frame for implementation, likely downtimes and breakdown of further costs (including training and licensing).

Consider using the following prior to making your final CRM purchasing decision:

- Select a CRM company that has a history of delivering success
- Create a shortlist of at least 3 to 5 vendors for your CRM evaluation
- Consider selecting a CRM vendor that understands your industry's unique business process
- Look for a vendor that offers good service training and support and treats you as though you are important to them
- Look for a product that's easy to use.
- Look at the longer term costs to ensure that you don't have to keep paying for extras
- Going with the cheapest CRM solution might cost more money in the long run
- If you need training on CRM, make sure the provider includes this in their service

Use the Database in Your Business, Specifically For Planning Your Telephone Sales Call Sessions

OK, so you've got your database and have transferred all your client records onto it.

You've had initial training on how to use the system (if needed) and are ready to go!

Your CRM system will allow you to fulfil a number of sales and marketing functions, running campaigns such as telemarketing, email marketing, text messages and sending letters, as well as making sure you don't forget those all important sales calls.

Making Those All-Important Telephone Sales Calls!

For this purpose, we are concentrating on planning the telephone sales session. This system is a real friend!

Firstly, create a group of contacts to phone, which can be defined by area (town or postcode), industry sector, source (e.g. from the networking activity you undertook to gain the client details)-you choose!

Enjoy Yourself - And Be a Winner

Ensure that the number of clients listed is reasonable for the time you are allocating to the session. Don't make the list too long, it will put you off! (Typically, you should aim to have 12 contacts to make for each hour you will be on the phone). This target is an achievable one, which allows for a combination of lengthy, productive calls with decision makers and those quick calls where you leave a message or agree to call back later. The target is based on the experiences of most good telemarketing companies who can make 100 calls in an 8-hour working day.

Make sure all the telephone numbers are included so that you can gain a real momentum when making those calls. As you speak to each client, record the outcome and follow up action and contact time (send email, phone back later, etc) on your system.

Target Marketing and Sales Campaigns with Mail Shots and Email

One of the key benefits of using a CRM system is that you can use it as the basis of communicating in a variety of ways to suit you and your customers. This is another key area for you to add to the list when having your initial training!

A Few Tips on Email Marketing

- Use good data (check that recipients have opted-in). Better still use your own data
- Keep messages simple and interesting – remember "less is more"

- Think about what people want and appeal to that, rather than what you want to sell
- If you use graphics, keep them simple too. You don't want your message to get lost
- A good subject line encourages people to open the email. Intrigue rather than sell
- Make sure it's easy to respond with a clear call to action and include an offline method of communication such as a telephone number
- Don't expect instant results from your first email – use it as a building process to encourage people to welcome your emails so they will open them and over time and take action
- Always create both html and plain text versions. Those who can't or choose not to receive html versions will still receive your message
- Track as much as you can, from open rates to clicks and final actions
- Test everything before you send it. It's much better to find out by test email that something is wrong or doesn't work than after you've sent it to a lot of other people

Conclusion

The benefit of installing a good, relevant database and updating your records on it cannot be overstated. By doing so, you *will* win new customers by getting closer to your prospective and existing customer's needs and having an effective system to ensure you take appropriate, timely action in contacting them!

You will also save time, giving those extra precious hours to get on and service existing clients, whilst ensuring your sales and marketing activity remains as effective as possible to win new customers.

> **MUST DO:** Always take business cards from people you meet or details from other sources (e.g. emails received) and put them in a simple spreadsheet to start with. All your client records must be in one place

Your database development checklist

> **MUST DO:** Always take business cards from people you lways take business cards from people you meet or

- ☐ Define your sales and marketing objectives
- ☐ What do you want to get out of the system-what is its purpose-list your requirements?
- ☐ Research the CRM services on the internet
- ☐ Choose your ideal system-match the CRM to your business needs-not the other way around!
- ☐ Buy and agree training sessions with your provider
- ☐ Gather all your client records
- ☐ Record details on your spreadsheet, using the correct fields or (recommended) populate your CRM system.
- ☐ Back up your database frequently (just as you do other information and systems).
- ☐ Create a contact group of prospects and clients
- ☐ Prepare for your sales calls by defining a number of clients to call. Keep the numbers manageable
- ☐ Get support and help on your sales campaign if needed.

Chapter One: Review

> **MUST DO:** Take time to prepare and practice your powerful introduction to the sales call-make sure it is based on benefits not features

Having read this chapter you have the tools of the trade to successfully start engaging in sales calls.

It is worth re-stating-the time you spend preparing for your calls is time well spent-don't rush it!

We have covered a great deal to prepare you physically and mentally for what is ahead.

I am often asked what would be the one thing I would focus on. I can tell you. It is getting your powerful introduction clear in your mind. Being able to say what you do in an engaging way, based on customer benefits not features will focus your mind on what it is you deliver and give you the confidence to engage with prospects at networking events and at the beginning of your sales call. Practice until your proposition rolls off your tongue!

Chapter Two

How to build effective relationships

A quick review of chapter one will remind you that you are now fully prepared to approach your prospect with a well prepared approach and powerful introduction. What could go wrong?

Objectives and Scope

- **Starting the sales call:** dealing with gatekeepers and getting to the decision maker on your side
- **Build Rapport/Fact Find:** Questioning techniques and listening skills to establish and agree customer needs.

You will be able to:

- Understand why the gatekeeper is there and why they won't put you through
- Engage them so that you stand the best chance of turning the gatekeeper into an ally; and
- Follow through the conversation to reach the person you need to speak to

Step iii): Starting the sales call

How to Engage with the Gatekeeper

We've all been there. You want to talk to someone and the person on the end of the call can't (or won't) put you through. The gate is closed. Sometimes it's bolted and guarded as well. You try all sorts of things to convince them that the person you really want to talk to will want to take your call. It hasn't worked and so you think ill of the person stopping you- the gatekeeper. But they're only human and if your call was important to the person they are 'protecting' what did you do wrong?

Getting past the gatekeeper is essential if you are to talk to the person who has the power to make the decision to buy your product or service (or at least to recommend it to the powers that be). How do you do it? Read on.

Understand Why the Gatekeeper Is There and Why They Won't Put You Through

You have prepared yourself for those sales calls and are ready to pick up the phone to talk to the decision makers.

Having got through to the right telephone number, the first person you speak to might not be the one you are seeking. A lot of the time you will be put through to the right person without a problem just by asking them, so don't start your call with the thought that you are going to come up against a gatekeeper as this could influence your tone and approach.

Sometimes the person on the end of the phone simply can't or won't put you through. We call these people "gatekeepers". They may take the guise of a receptionist, assistant, secretary or PA in the office, or husband/wife/partner. They are the one person stopping you from getting to the person you want to speak to, so it makes sense that we need to get the gatekeeper on our side.

As a first step, some people advocate that you should 'sell' to the gatekeeper on the basis that if they would buy what you are selling, then they'll put you through. This is true, up to a point. However, it might not be appropriate to relay all of the information you want the decision maker to hear to them.

We're not selling to the gatekeeper. We want to create enough interest for them to want to put you through to the right person.

Their objective will be to put through only those people who they think the person they are 'protecting' **will want to** speak to. Your objective is to help the gatekeeper understand that out of all the calls they receive, yours is the one that matters.

Think of it from their point of view. They receive so many poor business calls, that the gatekeepers are often irritated to death by calls from people who are unprepared and poor at communicating about what they do.

When they finally get a person on the phone, who is courteous, professional, has an interesting voice and a sense of humour, it's a refreshing change. Be like that and you will stand out.

Engage Them So That You Stand the Best Chance of Turning the Gatekeeper into an Ally

Smile before you pick up the phone...even when you don't feel like it. Try saying the sentence with a grimace and then with a broad smile. Your respondent at the end of the line can HEAR you beaming. That puts them (and you) in a more positive frame of mind.

You have now started the call in a friendly fashion which has you talking to them. You make your request to speak to Mr/Mrs decision-maker.

They won't, so you need to move on to the next stage.

Treat the gatekeeper like a new friend, but don't get too personal in the early stages of the call. Try to bring some humour or lightness into the conversation. Let them help you.

Take the time to establish rapport with each person you come in contact with. Whether or not they're the actual person you were wishing to speak to, they can help you achieve your desired result.

Here are some specific do's and don'ts:

- **Don't** assume the person is a gatekeeper - they might be a receptionist who is very busy or even someone who has just passed by the phone and picked it up. Stay positive and ask to be put through to the decision maker
- **Don't**, above all, be intimidated...they are just doing their job and may come across in a hostile manner (rare!) simply because they are busy and stressed. Their reaction isn't because of you!

- **Don't** say, "Are you having a good day?" or "How are you today?" This marks you out as a sales caller and one who is not really interested in the answer. After all why would you ring up someone you don't know and ask them how they are?
- **Do** find out their name and use it during the call (and any further ones)
- **Do** make your powerful introduction to them
- **Do** treat them as if they are a decision maker. They are, in so far as their decision to put you through is crucial
- **Do** show genuine interest in the person in terms of their business role. Ask for their help. For example, ask a question about the business that is relevant to your call ("How many staff do you have there?" or "Do you deal with xyz from that office?") to which they might know the answer. Ask questions to build rapport and find out what you need to know. You will soon find out if the business and the person you want to talk to is relevant to your sale and at the same time find out what you need to know about the business.
- **Do** make them feel important. Because they are!
- **Do** ask, when you judge the moment to be right, to be put through to the person you are seeking to speak to.
- **Do** ask to send information to them if they still can't or won't put you through, with a view to following up at an agreed date. See if you can get permission to cc the decision maker.

Most importantly, even above all this - be persistent.

"Persistence always overcomes resistance."

Gatekeepers admire people who won't give up, and if you're nice enough each time you call, they'll often finally fight on your side, for you to be put through.

A good approach is to call at different times if your initial attempts are rebuffed. Learn your decision maker's schedule.

Larger companies tend to have more gatekeepers than small ones, so you might need to employ a few different skills to get through to decision makers.

Here are some 'tricks of the trade' which you can use to get straight to the decision maker and avoid initial contact with the gatekeeper.

Tip 1

If you're persistently having trouble getting through but know that the decision maker will want to speak to you, and listen, yet you don't know their name...Try this.

Call the company. With a stern voice, ask to be put through to accounts payable. Since no one wants to handle a difficult customer looking for money, you'll invariably get put through. Plus, accounts people work in candle-lit caverns where no one else in the company talks to them and they feel very lonely.

Whoever in accounts answers laugh at the mistake and ask for the right person. The people in this department are often more compliant, and will more often than not, be happy to transfer you to the right person. You could even chat to the individual to get a little more information - but don't overdo it!

Tip 2

Another technique is to look at the number you have for the company. If the main number is, say 020 7999 2400, try 020 7999 2435, or two other random digits at the end. This is because most large companies have DDI ranges and ANYONE in the company is likely to be more helpful than the gatekeeper. When you get through, apologise, say you must have misdialled but could they put you through to your name contact direct. Some companies may be wise to this and put you back to the switchboard so it's best not to give your name at this stage.

Tip 3

If you 'do' know the person you want to speak to and you come across a gatekeeper...Try this.

"David Waved please…is he in?"

This often disarms them, and puts them in a situation where they can't say that David isn't in. It also sounds like you already know him, so gets you a step closer to being put through.

Tip 4

This is a variation of tip 3. Make sure you ask for the person in a friendly voice by their first name and last name (Fred Bloggs, not Mr Bloggs). It makes you sound like you already know them and can get you put through 'as a friend'. However, never say you are a friend, if the gatekeeper assumes, that's one thing, but don't lie.

OK –Think you've got it?

Well here's an example of how a sales call can go 'before' and' after' using these techniques.

Sophia was doing some telesales calls. She did a fair bit of cold calling, to sell drinks machines, but hadn't been trained or read this How to Guide.

The first call went like this:

Acme Widgets: Good morning, Acme Widgets, how can I help you?

Sophia: Can I speak to the proprietor of the business please?

AW: What's it about please?

Sophia: I want to talk to him about a new range of drinks machines we have on offer.

AW: Sorry, she won't be interested! Thank you! Goodbye!

End of conversation.

Sophia's complaint is "why can't they just have the decency to put me through?"

The next call went like this:

AW: Good morning, Acme Widgets, how can I help you?

Sophia: Yes this is Sophia, I wonder if you can help me?

(A psychological approach, starting in a positive frame, with "yes" and asking for help. People like to be able to help people. Saying 'this is' makes you sound important, like such as 'this is the Police.')

AW: I'll try!

S: Thank you. We've just launched a new range of money saving drinks machines, which are designed to keep your accounts department happy and reduce your operating costs, so I'd be grateful if you would put me through to the person who'd be interested in making some savings in this area.

(Here we've thanked the gatekeeper in advance, for helping out. Then we make him/her aware of the benefits to 'their' company that we're about to offer. We then tell him/her how grateful we'd be for their assistance, and draw on the fact that someone in the company is responsible for savings).

AW: She'll not be interested. We already have a cheap drinks provider, and they've not been in long.

S: I understand. Do you know how long the contract is?

AW: It's a 12-month contract.

S: That's fine. Many other people we talk to are in exactly the same situation, and what we've found, is that what we have to offer a greater range of drinks, keeping the staff happy, for less money overall, giving some savings for the company. They've found that once a company has them tied into a least cost service, they don't get to know about more beneficial services to the staff and to the bottom line. So even if you can't change now, would you agree that your company would benefit from knowing what's available, so they can save money in the future?

AW: Yes, I suppose you're right.

S: That's great, so can I ask who it is I need to speak to?

(Using 'can I' softens the blow of a direct question. You're more likely to get a positive response.)

AW: That would be Felicity Centricity.

S: That's great. Can you put me through to her please?

AW: Course I can!

See the difference?

It may not work every time but it will certainly help increase your success rate in getting through to the decision maker.

Overcoming Gatekeepers: The Voice Mail Addict

It's not unusual for a receptionist to inform you that the extension of the person you want to speak to is on voice mail and ask if you'd like to leave a message...?

Tricky one. Personally I'd either:

- Find out first from the receptionist whether it was this person's habit to leave voice mail on all the time or if I'd be likely to have more luck at another time - and if so, when?

  Or

- Politely refuse and try calling at various different times (just before business hours, lunch time and close of play are favourites)

However, if neither of these approaches gets you anywhere, you need to have a back up prepared:

1. Prepare a brief but convincing message with a call to action and a time when you will follow up this call – Use the powerful introduction you have prepared, then you can adapt it as necessary for each call.
2. If you still don't get through and the call is not returned, try sending an email including more information and a link to your company website. This is sometimes a more acceptable way to initially communicate with people who don't answer their phone, because they can reply without having to talk to you.
3. If no response to this route is received, you need to seriously question how important winning this company's business would be to you, as you have already invested quite a bit of valuable time and effort.
4. If you really want the business call the Managing Director's PA, explain the predicament and ask for their help. If they manage to get you through to your target, apologise to the MD and explain that you have been trying repeatedly without success to speak with the person you were seeking and why you wanted to speak with them in the first place.

Conclusion

So-are Gatekeepers real or imagined?

Well, did you ever see a job advert in your newspaper saying:

"Gatekeeper wanted-only aggressive people need apply'

Of course not!

In reality they are out there but often they only exist in our mind. The key to making a positive sales call is to assume, in the early stages that the person on the end isn't a gatekeeper. By approaching the call in the correct way, often you will be put through straight away.

If it becomes clear that you are talking to a gatekeeper, it is likely that they are actually performing a number of duties and tasks and pushing back sales calls is just one of them!

The way forward is to treat the person with respect, make them feel important and start to build a relationship with them. You will be able to do this by sharing a little bit about the potential solutions you can provide the company and asking relevant questions to build the relationship and your knowledge about the company.

The key is simple; prepare for the calls you make, stay positive and treat the person at the end of the telephone as a human being. Try a little humour along the way!

You're ready to go – here's your checklist

Your Gatekeeping checklist

> **MUST DO:** Have your powerful introduction including your benefit statement written down. This will help you in engaging with the gate keeper and decision maker.

1.	Be mentally prepared - assume that you will be put straight though to the decision maker.
2.	Be positive - smile as you dial to radiate that confidence!
3.	Prepare your introduction to the call, emphasising the benefits rather than the features of your service or product.
4.	Have questions ready that express an interest in their business. Make sure that the answer will be valuable to you in understanding the client's potential needs.
5.	Be prepared to take notes.

Step iii) Starting the sales call (continued)

How to get the decision maker on your side

Good preparation for your sales activity is vitally important to ensure maximum results are achieved from your sales calls. From the last section you will have been armed with this knowledge and now have the ability to overcome gatekeepers who may prevent you from talking to the decision maker.

From earlier chapters you will now have a:

- SMART objective for each of your calls; and
- A powerful introduction to your call

The next 60 seconds will set the tone for the call and have a major impact on the outcome. The introduction to the call is probably the most important part of the seven –step process. Get it right and you will get the customer talking about themselves and have a great opportunity to start understanding their needs. This will allow you to develop your sale effectively and make the other steps easy to climb!

In this section we will show you:

- How to create an immediate impact and develop your telephone call successfully
- How to achieve your objectives from the initial sales call to the customer

We will enable you to:

- Start your sales call in an effective and confident way
- Establish initial good rapport with the customer
- Understand how to develop the call to achieve your objectives-fact finding
- Plan the follow up to you call

Start Your Sales Call In an Effective and Confident Way

We have now got to the stage where you are now ready to talk to the decision maker. The receptionist and/or gatekeeper is putting you through and you are ready to talk to the decision maker.

The next 30 seconds will set the tone of the call and lay the foundations of whether the call is an effective one or not.

Here's the structure of your opening to the call:

- Ask a question which confirms you are talking to the decision maker (qualify the prospect)
- Make an opening benefit statement supported by a feature
- Ask a further question based on future plans for change which will get the customer talking

To start with, you may find it useful to have this as a script so that you can practice before calls are made. You may even wish to have this, or key points in front of you so that you feel in control. As you get into the swing of things, the opening to your calls will soon become second nature to you.

Tip: If you have a number of target markets, it may be useful to have a different content. Think and refer to your notes (This is where a good CRM system comes into its own —see the chapter earlier on How To Create And Use A Prospects Database For A Sales Campaign) to ensure your opening is relevant to the call every time.

The Introduction to the Call

Here's how the call could start, beginning with you introducing yourself:

> **Mike:** Hello, this is Mike White from CANsellWILLsell. Is that Mr Smith
>
> **Customer:** Yes - that's correct.
>
> **Mike:** Great. I understand that you are responsible for your company's xxx, is that right (Qualify the prospect).
>
> **Customer:** Yes thats right
>
> **Mike:** Ok - as I mentioned I'm calling from ABC and we help small businesses xxx). I'd like to see if we can help you too and am interested to know what you see as your key priorities are over the next few months. (Question based on future change).

From the above, you will see that the sales caller introduced the company name twice.

This works particularly well as it softens the start of the benefit statement and starts to embed the company name in the prospect's mind.

You can fine-tune this to reflect your own style and approach...and remember, you can adapt the introduction from experience over time!

Ask a Future Based Question

The future–based question might seem a bit presumptive; however, having got this far you will usually find that the prospect will give you at least a brief answer.

Try to avoid asking a question based on past experience. The prospect may express satisfaction, or give you information that doesn't help you progress the call. A question based on past experience runs the danger of getting into a lengthy discussion when you want to talk about the future. This would put you on the back foot.

Here's an example of a question based on past experience that goes nowhere:

> **Mike:**   **What have been your key priorities last year?**
>
> **Customer: Response**
>
> **Mike:**   **Were you successful?**
>
> **Customer: Very successful thank you.**
>
> **Mike:**   **??????**

By way of a summary,, get the introduction out of the way in under a minute and you've given the customer a chance to start talking about themselves. You've given them a brief overview of who you are and what you can do for them in terms of solving a problem or helping them take advantage of an opportunity.

Getting To the Fact Find – Building Rapport

The approach we've taken has the specific aim of getting you to the 3rd stage of the sale – building rapport and the Fact Find. This stage is important as it allows you to:

- Establish facts about the customer's business
- Establish their needs in relation to your offering.
- Build rapport with a sequence of questions and answers, observations and statements

In many cases, the customer will answer your question and this will lead directly into the Fact Find.

Barriers to Fact Finding

Sometimes, the response you receive will be unexpected. Such as:

- You are asked a question "What's it about?" "Tell me more about what you do?"
- Say they haven't got time to speak; or
- Indicate that they aren't interested

This is the first test of how well you have prepared. By being mentally and physically prepared, you can rise to this challenge. The key to success is to be positive and remember that your call is aimed at helping them.

During the course of your call, you may be told any number of things. You need to decide if these are genuine or not. To start with, assume they are and respond accordingly and aim to overcome any knock backs.

Remember not to get hung up on worrying about objections. Instead, look out for buying signals - in other words, signs of interest from the customer.

Buying signals come in different forms:

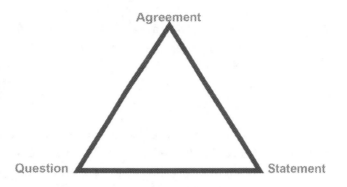

If asked a question, remain confident and positive by assuming it's a buying signal!

Here is an example of how you can keep your call on track and get you through any barriers to the Fact Find stage.

> **Question:** **What's it about?**
>
> **Answer:** **Well, we are helping companies like yours (use appropriate testimonials) to xxx.....We would like to do the same for you and I'd like to know a bit more about your company to see if we can. Can you tell me a little something of your challenges you may face in the next few months?**

See how the answer has assumed the question is a buying signal. We have answered it and asked another question to get the client talking and get the Fact Find back on track.

Tip: Have some testimonials from similar companies to hand, so that you can 'name drop' them if asked. This will support your claim that you are helping similar companies.

> **Statement:** **I haven't got time to talk at the moment.**
>
> **Answer:** **That's fine. I only need a couple of minutes to ask you about your business to find out if we can help you. Perhaps we can fit this in now or I can a call you when it's best for you.**

Here we have empathised, deflected the statement and assumed that the customer would be interested if he had time. We have managed expectations by indicating that the discussion will be a short one and given an option as to when to have a further discussion.

> **Statement:** **I'm not interested.**
>
> **Answer:** **That's fine. I can understand how you may not wish to discuss this with me as we haven't met before. I'm just keen to see if there is an opportunity to help you increase your staff motivation and retention, as we have with other similar companies (as above-name them!).**
>
> **........a couple of questions will help me to find out if we can help you too-If not, I will be on my way ! (Introduces modest humour, if appropriate).**
>
> *Or, if you are not comfortable with this, something like*
>
> **.......and a brief discussion with you will allow us to assess whether this is the case.**

Again, we have empathised, deflected the statement, reassured the customer about the context of the call and asked a question to get them talking about their business. We have also tested whether the prospect really hasn't got time or is trying to "fob you off".

Top Tip: After all of this, if you are getting nowhere with the customer and they say they are not interested, don't worry, and move onto your next call.

Have one last go. If you deem it worthwhile, what have you got to lose having got this far?

Here are two questions you can ask; choose whichever is relevant to your discussion.

1) "OK, that's fine Mr Smith. Can I ask what in particular you don't feel comfortable with?"

2) "OK, I can see what it is you mean. When would it be best to contact you again to see if your situation has changed?"

This will give you one final chance to keep the call alive but more likely, it means you will leave the call feeling you have had feedback and have not been rejected.

If after all that, it's still a "'no", remember:

SW	SW	SW	SW
Some will	Some won't	So what?	Someone's waiting

Its part of the process of qualifying the prospect as not everyone you call on your list will need your product or service and not everyone is a good fit for what you are offering. You are looking for those who need your help.

The Fact Find

Once you have got by the opening, you're successfully through to the start of the Fact Find!

At this stage, you will have started building rapport with the customer and commenced a dialogue within which you will have both learned something about each other's business. It's up to you to build on this rapport, establish the customer's needs and gear yourself to getting to the 'sales' stages of the call.

Mike White

This means asking more questions and remembering the established piece of advice:

You have two ears and one mouth-listen twice as much as you speak.

What Type Of Questions Should You Ask?

The first answer to this may sound obvious - ONLY ask questions you want to know the answers to!

So often, it can be tempting to fill gaps in discussion or try to build rapport with questions that have no relevance to what you are trying to achieve from the call.

Try not to do this. The questions will sound insincere and may annoy the person at the end of the phone because it comes over as time wasting.

Open and Closed Questions

There has been a lot of advice over the years about the best use of open and closed questions.

Let's look at this again:

Closed questions: These will lead to a "Yes" or "No" answer.

Example: "Do you have a staff pension scheme at present?"

Open Questions: These will provoke a lengthier, sentence based response.

Example: "What are your plans for reviewing you pension benefits over the next few months?"

Sometimes, open questions may still evoke a "Yes/No" answer, just presented differently!

Here's an example:

Question: "What are your plans for reviewing you pension benefits
over the next   few months?"

Answer: "We don't have any"

That's the same as saying "No" to a closed question. This doesn't matter,
just be aware that the type of question you ask should be asked for particular
reasons and should be chosen carefully.

Practice your questions on someone you trust to give real feedback before
the call is made. This is a good reality check and should build your
confidence however, do not assume that everyone will answer with the
same words, so look for the meaning.

Closed Questions

These are used when you want to clarify or establish the customer's need.

They can also guide the response to the answer you are looking for,
providing the question is asked in the correct way!

Take a look at the following use of closed questions. The second one is
more likely to achieve the more beneficial response for you.

- "So, from what you have told me, you would like to improve your
  profile within local media over the next three months. Have I got
  this right?" *Answer could be "yes or no"*
- "So, from what you have told me, you would like to improve your
  profile within local media over the next three months. That's right
  isn't it?" *You are leading the person to a "Yes" answer, which is the
  one you want?*

Open Questions

These are really useful when you are trying to understand needs and obtain
information. Typical words used to start an open question are:

- Who
- What
- Where
- When
- Why
- Which
- How

What should you be asking? Use these openings in relation to your own business and conversations you've had with customers in order to build questions. Again, test them out on someone.

A key to your success will be your ability to ask questions that confirm in the customer's mind a need, problem or opportunity in the future, which you can help with. Try to get answers you know will allow you to present your service as a solution to what has been said.

> **Examples**
>
> **Question:** **What is your current staff turnover compared to your target?**
>
> **Question:** **In which areas of your business do you anticipate employing new members of staff?**

TOP Tip: When developing your Fact Find, remember that it isn't an interrogation!

Be interesting and sound interested in what you are being told. Make the session conversational by using link words and phrases and when appropriate, use a little humour.

"Do you know, that's really interesting? Can you tell me more about…"

"I'm not sure I understand that…. it must be Monday (!).. are you saying that…."

Tip: Take hand written notes during the call.

This will allow you to keep a reminder of what has been said so you can use the information or to put into your database for future calls. Avoid inputting notes directly onto your computer – the customer will hear you tapping the keyboard and might think they don't have your full attention. This will ensure that the person at the end of the phone isn't aware that you are taking notes or being distracted.

You have now spent a few minutes developing a really good rapport and have established some interesting and relevant facts about the customer. You should now have enough information to be able to start selling to the prospect.

However, don't jump in just yet!

Consolidate the Fact Find - Confirm the Need.

Even the most experienced sales people often forget to consolidate the Fact Find. To do this, we need to get from them:

- Agreement as to what they have said
- A commitment as to their needs
- A wish to do something about it

"So, Mr Smith what you are saying is that you are looking to increase your client base by 15% and are currently reviewing your website and email campaigns. Have I got that correct?"

Do you see how the closed question is used to confirm the need?

This ties the customer in and gets their commitment to you. You've now achieved a huge buying signal and got the customer used to saying "yes" to you!

Looking Out For Needs

During you conversation, the customer will say things that will help make your sales call easier. They will indicate their needs; you need to understand and capture this information effectively and use it when you consolidate your Fact Find.

They might express their needs in one of 2 ways:

- Explicitly: A clear, unambiguous statement about wants, desires and intentions. It is easy to capture these, just listen and make a note of them
- Implicitly: This is any statement by the customer that says they are dissatisfied with the current situation. With a general statement like this you need to ask further 'open ended 'questions until they state their need explicitly or where you can reflect back to confirm the need in your own explicit closed question

Prepare and Plan the Follow Up To the Call

Congratulations, you have established rapport with the customer and have agreed what their needs are for the future. To get this far, you probably had opportunities to say something about your company, what you offer and how you have helped others, thus establishing credibility.

Where to from here?

The next stages of the sales process, which you might be able to cover in your call, are to:

- Present your product; and
- Make a specific recommendation to the client based on their needs

Whilst for most calls (especially ones in which you are speaking to the decision maker for the first time), you will probably have made a SMART objective to get an appointment to enable you to present. You might be able to go further.

If you feel that the call is going well and you are able to address the customer's needs there and then, keep the call going and move on to presenting your service or product and close the deal. Strike whilst the iron is hot and you have the customer's attention! We cover these steps in Chapter three.

If this isn't the case and a meeting is needed to close the call successfully, finish the consolidation (i.e. agree client needs) and suggest to the customer that you meet to go through your proposal.

Having got their agreement in principle, ask when would be convenient and get it in your diary. Also ask for the email address so that you can confirm the meeting.

Following the call, email the customer to thank him or her for their time on the phone and to confirm the time and place of the meeting. To avoid confusion on the day, it is also useful to include a very brief summary of your discussions, including their agreed needs and the reason for the meeting.

TOP TIP: Sometimes a customer may ask for written details to be sent rather than having a meeting. If you feel this is appropriate, gain agreement as to how the information should be sent (e.g. email, post).

A key to maintaining control in this situation is to ensure that you agree a date when you can re-contact the person to discuss the information you send. Make sure you keep to the appointed time.

Finally, make sure that any notes you have made are summarised and inputted onto your database/CRM system for future reference.

Conclusion

Making a good sales call is all about preparation, understanding the customer's needs and satisfying them.

You now have the tools and techniques to prepare for the call and to make that all-important powerful introduction.

Having established rapport with the customer, you will be able to find out a lot of information about them. Within this, by making sure you note the key needs of the customer and getting them to agree these, you are well on the way to being able to make a powerful presentation (either face to face or on the telephone) and satisfy their needs. In other words...to make a sale!

Checklist

- ☐ Review preparation
- ☐ SMART objective in place
- ☐ Powerful introduction (script or bullet points) on desk
- ☐ Stay positive and treat any customer reaction as either feedback or a buying signal, not rejection!
- ☐ Build rapport
- ☐ Fact Find using open questions
- ☐ Consolidate the Fact Find using closed questions
- ☐ Take notes during the call
- ☐ Agree timing and objectives of the next meeting

Or

- ☐ Present your proposal and close the deal (Chapter three shows you how!)
- ☐ Summarise notes after the call session on your database/CRM system
- ☐ Confirm next meeting (or sale) in writing
- ☐ Follow up action

Chapter Two: Review

OK. So you've spent some time developing a really good rapport and have established some interesting and relevant facts about the customer. You should now have enough information to be able to get to actually selling to the prospect.

MUST DO: My top tip for this chapter is the same as for Chapter one- make sure that you understand fully your customer proposition that you can now explain in under a minute. In working out your powerful introduction you will probably have a list of features and benefits that aren't included in your introduction. Have these listed so that you can answer questions and develop dialogue as your fact find progresses

Chapter Three

How to present and close the deal

Objectives and scope

In this chapter we show you how to:

- make the most of opportunities when you get to meet prospective customers face to face
- Gain skills and techniques to be confident and prepared when you meet prospects in a range of situations
- Deliver powerful PowerPoint presentations

You will be able to:

- Prepare physically and mentally to see prospective customers
- Handle a variety of situations that occur in sales meetings
- Understand various questioning techniques to develop rapport and identify the customer's needs
- Develop your Fact Find to maximise your chances of getting an order
- Conduct effective meetings and deliver powerful PowerPoint presentations
- Undertake successful negotiations and close the sale

To re-cap, you have now fully engaged with the prospect and know enough about his needs and requirements to actually start selling.

You have the tools and techniques to close the deal by either:

- Continuing your sales call on the telephone

Or

- Conducting an agreed sales meeting at a later date

Either way you have now reached the latter steps of the sales process. This is when you present your company and services more fully, make a specific recommendation based on the prospects needs and close the deal.

To recap, to get this far you have:

i)   Prepared for the introductory sales call
ii)   Successfully completed the introductory telephone sales call, overcoming the gatekeeper (if necessary) and gained engagement with the client.
iii) Gained confirmation of his/her needs; and
iv)   Agreement to take the discussion (sales process) further and get to the presentation stage, either during this meeting or at a future date

If you feel that the call is going well and you are able to address the customer's needs there and then, keep the call going and move on to presenting your service or product. Strike while the iron is hot, while you have the customer's attention and close the deal, we cover how to complete the sale later in the chapter

Should your sales approach require a face to face meeting, read on for some great tips on conducting a great sales meeting. If not turn to page xxx and join us again to learn how to complete the sale.

Step vi) Presentation

How to conduct an Effective Sales Meeting

We now know that making a good sales call is all about preparation, understanding the customer's needs and satisfying their needs.

Physical & Mental Preparation

Freshness

Before you enter the customer's premises and introduce yourself to the receptionist (in larger companies) or the client, a final check is in order!

Phrases like "first impressions last" and "you only get one chance to make a first impression" must be your mantra. Research into job applicants suggests that 80% of interviewers make their decision about offering someone a job in the first 7 seconds that they see an interviewee.

Freshness applies in a mental and physical sense.

Mental Freshness

The obvious:

- Make sure you don't have a big night out the night before
- Don't book too many appointments into one day if you are doing this on successive days

Physical Freshness

Sometimes an embarrassing subject but it needs to be dealt with. Here is a checklist

Look good from the neck up:

- Keep your hair cut, combed (if appropriate), and tied back
- Not too much make-up for the ladies, clean-shaven ideally for the men
- If you wear glasses, think whether the ones you wear give the right impression to prospects

Breath:

- Drinking water regularly helps to keep your breath fresh
- Address the obvious issues around dental hygiene

- Carry mints with you but finish sucking them well before the meeting. Over-minty breath can almost be as over-powering as halitosis!

Clothing:

- Follow the rule that you should dress as the particular prospect EXPECTS you to dress
- Some sales people carry a fancy tie and a boring tie plus a jumper (for males) so that they can change their attire chameleon-like to suit the environment on prospect
- If your job takes you onto building sites, make sure you have suitable site wear

Fragrance

- Too much can be as off-putting as body odour

Smoking/drinking/chewing gum

- No amount of masking will hide these habits from prospects that don't appreciate them

Call of Nature

- This will also give you time to make a final visual check of your appearance

Distractions

Mobile phones should be turned off. Not set to silent. Get into the habit of checking the phone the moments before you walk into the appointment.

If their phone keeps ringing or people keep coming into the room to ask questions of the appointee, have the confidence and self-respect to ask for their undivided attention. A good, inoffensive phrase is:

"I can see that a lot of people need to get hold of you today. Would you prefer if we met at another time?"

Be prepared if they say "yes" and reappoint. Alternatively, they might take the hint and close the door or put their phone on divert. Some appointees will reassure you that it is not a problem for them; so just plough on.

Materials

- Pens: take at least two spares into the meeting with you
- Pad: ideal is a quality leather folder with A4 pad. It makes you look professional and prepared
- Marketing materials: the meeting is about you and the prospect so, marketing materials can be distracting. Generally, use marketing materials in your follow-up. They may be keen to see these and you can use this as an excuse to follow-up, should you need it

Venue

It is always better to meet a prospect on neutral ground or in your offices. But this is rarely possible. You want to take a "controlling" position wherever possible and if given the opportunity, to prepare the meeting room:

- Avoid sitting behind a desk
- Position the seating so that you can interact in a business like, but engaging way The prospect must also be able to easily view presentation materials you may be showing
- Have "one more person" than them: if you can bring a specialist with you (by prior agreement) and the prospect is alone, this is ideal

When you meet a decision maker at their premises:

- Try to sit at 90% to the prospect rather than the other side of a barrier such as a desk. If there is a meeting table or coffee table, opt for that rather than sitting opposite their desk
- Ensure you are both seated rather than walking or standing;;you are likely to get a longer meeting

- Avoid low chairs and adjust the chair as necessary to raise your height and fix any reclining features
- Spend as much time getting clues from bookshelves, awards, photographs, etc. about their non-work life and interests

Welcome & Rapport

Upon meeting the prospect, shake hands and make sure you have your card to hand over. By giving them your card at that point, it can overcome any potential embarrassment if they forget your name (it has happened).

Rapport is shorthand for "building the relationship". People buy from people they like, as we have outlined earlier. So, let's look at the issues and techniques specific to building rapport in a face-to-face sales meeting.

Find points of commonality. By now, you should have picked up clues about the prospect as a person. Family pictures will give you an idea of the age of their children. If it matches the ages of your children, this is a powerful point of commonality. If there is a picture of them with a large fish and you like fishing, get stuck in talking about tackle.

Talk about what the prospect likes. If they have golf trophies and you know about golf, raise it as an early discussion point. If there are books on management theory and you recognise one, use it as a discussion point.

Engage in small talk. There is a real art in conducting small talk without sounding like you are just trying to fill in time. In some cultures, the parties will get straight down to business. If the prospect is busy, they similarly will shun the small talk. Be very alert to the likelihood that they might chat in an unstructured way or might be more direct. You can get an idea by talking to their secretary, assistants or colleagues. You can even ask them directly: you will be surprised how helpful these "influencers" can be if you engage in small talk with THEM!

The conversation might start with a discussion of your journey. Don't dismiss this by simply saying "fine"; let the conversation flow naturally.

Drinks and Food

Socially and subconsciously, it is important to accept any offer of drinks. Even if you are not thirsty! Try to have the same drink as the prospect, for example coffee if you can see they drink coffee.

Reject offers of food such as biscuits. They can be messy, distracting and your mouth might be full if you get asked a question.

Keep Control

If it becomes necessary, be sure that you are the person that says "well, I know you are busy, do you mind if I bring the conversation back to why I am here". It is all very well getting on like a house on fire and discovering you have shared parentage but you need to make sure you have time to sell to them!

Always have an agenda/structure as to how you want the meeting to go – lead, don't follow. See later.

Eye Contact & Body Language

You are there to get as much information out of the prospect as possible. To this end, you need to physically look interested. It is not enough to just BE interested.

You can do this by keeping as much eye contact as possible with the prospect. But avoid staring! It is a skill to balance this with careful note taking. Prioritise eye-contact over the note-taking. If the prospect is obviously shy and does not respond with good eye contact, take a less confrontational position.

This can be achieved by using occasional glances whilst directing the prospect to look at presentation materials and other tools to reduce the need for the prospect to give you constant visual attention.

Progressing the Meeting

Have a structure

The best meetings have a logical structure that everyone can follow and that leads to a conclusion. Yours might differ slightly depending upon the purpose of the meeting, but here is an outline:

- Confirm the parameters
- Set the tone of the meeting (inc. note taking)
- Question – Fact Finding
- Review/consolidate
- Repeat 2 above as required
- Summarise needs/test close as required
- Present solution
- Close or move to next stage

Confirm the Parameters

You may be surprised how often meetings are well underway before the parties realise there was confusion over the reason for the visit. At the beginning of the meeting, be confident and ask for agreement on:

- The reason for the meeting (have the confirmation email you sent prior to the meeting to hand to remind the prospect, if needed, of the purpose)
- The duration: when is the latest you can finish by? Or say, "Shall we aim to finish by….?"
- The likely outcome: for example you want enough information to submit a detailed proposal by next week

Set the Tone

You want to be business like both for their sake and for yours.

Ask permission to make notes. Why?

- This shows that you are serious about taking down the information
- You ensure information is accurately captured
- You can refer to it through the meeting to make sure you stay on track
- It makes it clear to the prospect that it is up to them to do the talking

The Fact Find - Questioning Skills

Consider yourself a detective or a doctor. It is your job to find out as much about the person in front of you as possible so that the best assessment can be made. To do this, you need to ask powerful questions.

In general, for face-to-face meetings you want the prospect to talk unencumbered. The best tools for this are "Open" questions. These are questions that are difficult to answer "yes" or "no" to such as those beginning with the words:

- When
- Where
- Who
- How
- Why
- What

If specific information is required, you need to check something or if want to close down the conversation at the end of the meeting, you need to use questions that are more easily answered "yes" or "no".

Questions beginning with the following words fall into this category and are called "Closed" questions:

- Do/Does
- Is/Are
- Can/Can't

Generally, prospects find it easier to give answers to closed rather than open questions.

Open and closed questions can be sub-classified into "Opinion" and "Factual" questions. Some questions ask people what they feel or think about something – opinion questions. Others are not a matter of opinion and most people asked that question would give the same answer such as "How many inches are in a foot?" These are factual questions.

This table illustrates how the two styles of question combine.

	Opinion	*Factual*
Closed	Neither difficult nor easy	Easy
Open	Difficult	Neither difficult nor easy

At the beginning and end of the meeting you should stick to easy questions. The hardest questions to answer such as "who are you likely to ask to do this business?" or "how much would you like to spend?" are Open Opinion questions and are best sandwiched in the middle of the meeting.

Consolidate the Fact Find - Keep Clarifying Points

We covered this earlier when discussing how to effectively engage with the prospect and gain initial agreement of their needs. Having now developed the Fact Find and gained valuable information about the customer's future needs and/or opportunities, you will be thinking about how you can deliver solutions for these later or at the next the client needs again here meeting. Consolidating and agreeing the client's needs will give you a great platform for this

Make clear notes of the verbal and non-verbal responses obtained from the prospect. This will not only guide your continued pitch at that meeting but also make it more likely that your follow-up gets a good reception from the decision maker(s).

This is part of controlling the meeting. Keep referring to your notes and make sure you are clear about what the prospect has said. Rephrase any concepts of which you are unclear and feed that back to the prospect. Don't be shy to use this process to uncover sales opportunities and requirements that were not previously agreed as discussion points. Don't get sidetracked

– stick to the primary purpose but work hard to return to those additional opportunities that you have uncovered later in the meeting.

Once you believe you have enough information to present suitable products/ services and solutions, recap the key observations made and the conclusions you have come to. This gives the customer an early chance to get into the habit of saying "yes" to you. More importantly, it ensures that you will go into the presentation stage with their specific needs agreed and tested.

> **Example**
>
> **You are a solicitor, providing Human Resources legal support**
>
> **"Thank you for sharing your current situation Peter, and for discussing your future plans with me.**
>
> **If I have got it right, it sounds like you are looking to undertake a number of redundancies within the next 12 months. Is that right?"**

Presentation

If it is appropriate to show presentation materials (e.g. example product or sales literature), try to ensure that they are subtly out of sight until needed. Depending on what you are selling, you might not need them at all. This will minimise the chance of the customer being distracted and allow you to maintain control.

When presentation material is required, make sure that you show it! Make an effort to put the information in front of the customer (for example, don't have sales information facing you. Look at it and refer to it upside down if necessary - you should know it by heart anyway!).

If appropriate, walk around to the customer and look at the detail of your presentation material side by side. This can be a powerful way of engaging with the customer and deflecting eye contact if they are shy.

Test Closes

Throughout the meeting, you can also gauge the enthusiasm of the prospect to the various options by trying test closes. These are lines that are a rephrased version of true closes but mean you help the prospect to reach a conclusion. Here are some sample test closes a Financial Adviser might use:

- "If we could do the financial review within the next four weeks, would that suit you?"
- "What sort of monthly income do you think you will need when you retire?"
- "If we could generate the income you need and a lump sum, would that be of interest?"

Wrapping Up

Always make time to go over what you have discussed. This avoids any confusion as to the outcomes of the meeting and makes you look professional and in control.

Agree what you will send (if anything) and the deadlines. Give yourself plenty of time. Don't be press-ganged into a rapid follow-up. Much rather, get the answers to the questions raised and allow for posting.

Gain permission from the prospect to contact them by telephone to "get their feedback" around a specified duration after they receive the proposal or follow-up material.

When They Say "Yes"

Remember that you are going to the meeting in order to win the business. On rare occasions, the appointee will make a purchasing decision at the meeting.

Be optimistic and be prepared for this. If you need order forms, take them with you to the meeting and fill them in there and then. Be sure to get that all important signature.

Alternatively, you or they may need sales order or purchase order numbers respectively. Make the call to the relevant departments if necessary and get this pinned down there and then if you can.

Depending on how the call ends and time constraints, this can be a great time to ask for a referral-don't miss out on the opportunity!

When They Say "No"

Sometimes the prospect will tell you at the end of the meeting that they don't believe you can meet their requirements. Remember the purpose of the meeting is for both parties to decide whether there is business that can be done. This means that sometimes it can't be done. Take it on the chin and move on.

Top Tip: Remember, we should try to treat rejection in a positive way. One way to do this is to treat it as feedback and learn from it.

Also remember to establish if your product /service could be appropriate in the future, especially if you were to modify it, in line with the client's observations.

Keep the door open!

Example

"**Thank you for your time Mr Smith. I can see that our service isn't right for you just now as we can't xxxx. However, we are consistently reviewing our range of services in response to customer feedback. Should they develop so that they meet your requirements, is it ok to call you again?**"

Other Top Tips & Tricks

Keep an Eye on the Time

Ideally, avoid doing this in an obvious way. Looking up at a wall clock or checking your wristwatch might both remind the prospect that they have limited time or wrongly indicate to them that you are bored.

If you have the time to over-run, don't remind the prospect of the agreed end time! If you have a tight schedule, make sure that you wrap in time for clarification of your discussion and goodbyes.

Decision Making Unit

You may find out during the course of the meeting that the person in front of you is not (or not the only) decision maker. Be very wary of pitching to this person further.

If you find out it is another investor, another department head, the husband, etc, ask if they can join you in the meeting now. If you think it is appropriate and you have the confidence, maybe even suggest that you keep the meeting brief and rearrange for a time when the other members of the decision making unit can be present.

If this is not done, you will often find that your follow-up, proposal or pitch at the end of the meeting falls on deaf ears. This will only delay the buying process and reduce your credibility. Arguably, you should know even before the appointment was secured that the person in front of you was not the true decision maker. In reality, this will often not become apparent until you are eyeball to eyeball.

If it is obvious they have no requirement get out. Don't waste their time or yours and move on.

Before you get out, make sure you leverage their time.

- Ask them for referrals. If they are a nice person, they will feel a certain guilt and obligation that you have made the effort to visit,

so ask them if they know someone who might be a good prospect. Don't be shy to push for an actual introduction be certain that there is no potential need in the future. If there might be, then get a timescale
- Can you get referrals for contacts of yours? This might seem bizarre but you can generate good will and return referrals if you find out that they need a good solicitor and you happen to know one. It's a long shot, but if you don't ask, you don't get!

After The Meeting

Your follow-up should be clear and obvious because you agreed it at the meeting wrap-up.

It is better to post nicely-presented follow-up material in branded folders. However, some prospects will prefer email, so consider sending both. If you do email, send it in PDF format rather than Microsoft Word or Excel because it will appear on their screen exactly as you intended. Otherwise formatting issues and incompatibilities with PCs can mess things up. You can get a free PDF converter on the Internet. A good search engine should serve well here. Try searching for a "free PDF converter".

Don't assume the prospect has received or read your carefully-crafted proposal. In many cases they will need persistent chasing and reminding and you should not be shy about doing this. They will feel slightly morally obliged so will tolerate a higher level of follow-up than with a telephone discussion.

Conclusion

You now have a wealth of information and techniques to use at a meeting. Practice each group of techniques and you will find that they soon start to come naturally. But don't beat yourself up if you forget an element. Even the best sales people forget something.

Great meetings are an art and come through practice. Accept that you will have many that do not result in business. However you may well have gone a long way to improving your chance of winning business in the future by sowing seeds of thought with the prospect and by having built a relationship.

**People do business when they want to
buy - not when you want to sell!**

More importantly, whilst your key objective from your first meeting may have been to reach agreement on a deal, you will often find that other SMART objectives, (which will make you feel you have come out a winner!) are just as valuable to achieve

Establish and agree the client's needs and opportunities

Understand when these are going to be reviewed and actioned in the future

Gain agreement for you to meet again, on a specific date to discuss your service and put forward a specific proposal based on your discussions

The success formula is a simple one:

Good Preparation + Effective Questioning & Listening Skills =Potential Success

Checklist

> **MUST DO: In the meeting listen more than you talk by asking relevant questions. Be yourself and don't panic-rejection isn't life threatening and someone will say 'YES'**

SW	SW	SW	SW
Some will	**Some won't**	**So what?**	**Someone's waiting**

Prepare

- Be mentally fresh
- Be physically fresh
- Check your appearance

- Have your materials to hand
- Turn your phone off

Welcome & Rapport

- **Look for pointers to areas of commonality to engage in small talk and build rapport.**

Progressing the Meeting

- Have a structure
- Confirm the parameters
- Set the tone
- Undertake the Fact Find using your questioning skills
- Take notes
- Consolidate & clarify points
- Present your proposal or next steps
- Test close or close

Wrap Up

- Recap
- Agree follow-up actions
- Agree deadlines

After The Meeting

- Follow-up as agreed

Step iv) Presentation (continued)

How to use PowerPoint for successful presentations

Oh no-not death by PowerPoint!

In the last section you were given the tools to conduct an effective sales meeting, including tips on presenting to a small group of two or three people.

Sometimes we are invited to present to a much larger audience which requires a different, more dynamic approach-with PowerPoint often having an important role to play.

Here's some good news!

Being a good PowerPoint presenter is not something you are born with. People say "I am lucky that I was born with great communication skills." This is nonsense. No-one is born a great PowerPoint presenter, you aren't born charismatic, you don't pop out of the womb saying "and on the next slide you will see........"

As a result, you might have watched many boring PowerPoint presentations that have given rise to the phrase "Death by PowerPoint!" 30 million PowerPoint presentations are being given every day so it's a skill well worth mastering.

Being good with PowerPoint and presenting is something that you can learn, something that with a little practice and time you can become very good with. This guide will help you to captivate, intrigue and make presentations even more memorable than before.

You might even start to enjoy using PowerPoint!

Objectives and Scope

In this chapter we provide a process that will allow you to create stunning PowerPoints that entertain, inform and engage. This process will allow you to make your message stand out amongst the thousands of others we are exposed to every day.

Following this simple process will build massive confidence for your next presentation.

After reading this section you will be able to:

1. Understand the reason for using PowerPoint
2. Control what the audience sees and when
3. Make your presentations more memorable by using PowerPoint
4. Get your message across easier and quicker than ever before
5. Design great looking slides
6. Deliver dynamic presentations

Why Use PowerPoint?

PowerPoint has a bad reputation; undeserved in my view. It stems from poorly trained people using it and now some people in the presentation skills training industry are even warning you not to use it.

So why should you bother with this piece of software?

There are several very good reasons:

- A picture equals a thousand words – it can take you ten minutes to explain to an audience what a picture can show in just a few short seconds
- It adds impact – used properly, your audience's attention can be easier to keep
- It aids memory retention – by engaging more of the participants' senses, visual, auditory and kinaesthetic, you are making your presentation more memorable
- It appeals to all different types of learners – some audience members want to hear things, some have to see them and some only take it in by doing it. By using PowerPoint, you appeal to more of the learning styles in the audience
- It can get complex ideas across quickly – It can help you to get over complex structures and relationships far quicker than just words
- It can be a lot of fun

Planning an Effective PowerPoint

Confidence and smooth delivery comes from two things in presenting:

- Preparation
- Practise

You may have seen slick PowerPoint presentations before that have great visuals and smooth transitions between looking at the slides and the presenter communicating with us. You may have thought "wow I bet that took hours to put together". Well there is no substitution for preparation and practise but we can show you how to make a visually stunning slide deck quickly and easily.

Allow yourself the time and resources to prepare and practice for your next PowerPoint and you will be astounded by the results. We put so much pressure on ourselves to deliver brilliant presentations with little preparation and practice, no wonder we get stressed when we present!

The following steps can be used quickly as a guide to creating a great PowerPoint presentation that will enhance your message and make it more memorable.

Follow these simple steps and we will get you on the road to powerful PowerPoints with confidence and charisma.

Presentation Objectives

The first step, before even getting near a computer, is to know the objective of your talk. What do you want people to think, feel or do differently after you have finished talking. You must have a clear objective for the presentation. For more information on Objectives please read our Guide "How to Deliver an Effective Presentation".

Secondly, you must have all your ideas down on paper and have formulated your speech. We recommend using mind mapping to do this. You can find out more about mind mapping and idea generation in the Guide we just referred to. The areas that we suggest that you have covered are:

- Stories
- Information
- Statistics
- Objectives

- Audience
- Topical news items
- Benefits

Make sure you have written your speech before you get anywhere near a laptop or PC. Then ask yourself these questions:

1. Do I need PowerPoint presentation to demonstrate my point?
2. Can I enhance my message with the use of visual aids?

If the answer to these questions is "no", then don't use PowerPoint.

If the answer is "yes", then we will start by creating a wire frame overview of our presentation on PowerPoint. Before we do that, let's look at what makes a bad PowerPoint so that we can avoid those mistakes when putting one of our own together.

The Six Biggest PowerPoint Mistakes

These are the top PowerPoint mistakes people make time and time again. Avoid these and you are most of the way there:

- **Reading the slides** –Never read from the slides when presenting. If you had everything to say on your slides then, we wouldn't need you! You could have sent it to me and I could have read it for myself in bed with a mug of cocoa.
- **Facing the slides** – When you turn your back on the audience you lose your rapport and connection with the audience. The connection is lost and your presentation is dead.
- **Too much information** – If you have too much information on the slide, people will try to decipher what it is rather than listening to what you are saying. Too much information can distract the audience and take away from your presentation.
- **Too much text** – If the audience is reading your slides, then they are not listening to you. Half the audience will be listening to you and half reading. Everyone will form different ideas and your message will be diluted.
- **Standing in front of the slide** – You have taken the time to make slides. Let your audience see them. People will be thinking

about what they are missing out on and won't hear a word of what you say.

- **Using it as a memory aid** – You have created a talk starting with the slides and are only using them so that you know what to say next. When the slide changes, you turn around and look confused for a second before saying "Ah, yes that is what I wanted to say". Are you taking this presentation seriously enough? Do you care if you get the business? Do you care what the audience thinks of you?

Avoid these 6 major mistakes and you are well on your way to a decent PowerPoint before we have even started.

Wire Frame Creation

You have created your speech, know what you are going to say and have decided to use PowerPoint to enhance the presentation. What next?

The first step is to create a text wire frame of the presentation to which you can then add visuals. To do this, open PowerPoint and create some blank slides, then put the different sections of your talk as titles:

This creates the basic structure into PowerPoint and then will allow you to change from the traditional PowerPoint view to the slide sorter view. This can be achieved by pressing "alt+w" followed by "I" or by using the "view menu" and clicking "slide sorter".

This is what you will see:

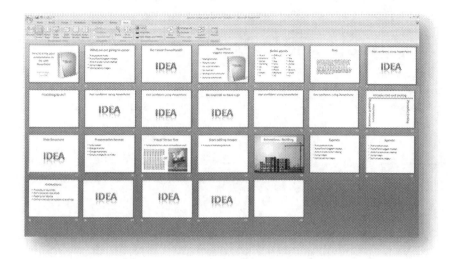

You will have a clear overview of the message title by title, slide by slide. This will allow you to see from a high level how the chunks fit together. You can then easily move around slides in the deck to get the desired structure. Simply drag and drop the slides into place. The slide sorter is a great view for getting the structure sorted before getting down to the detail of each individual slide.

Create a wire frame overview of all your slides first. Don't worry about formatting as we can change all the title formatting in one go later on, after we have sorted out the structure. For more information on structuring your presentation, read our Guide "How to Deliver an Effective Presentation".

Slide Formatting Made Easy

There is a quick way to change fonts for titles and the entire layout of the slides in the deck using "View menu" and "Slide Master". This makes it so easy to make sweeping changes throughout the presentation.

It does come with a disclaimer though. If you have built all of your slides and then decided to change the font, there may be some formatting issues. This is because different fonts have varying sizes and lengths. The text may jump down lines and do funny things. It is always better to do your formatting in the early stages after creating the wire frame before working for too long on the specific design of individual slides.

To make changes, go to "View" then to "Slide Master". The best slide to make changes to is the very first slide. By changing this slide, it changes all of the other slides in the deck. Click the first slide at the top of the slide panel at the left, make your formatting changes and then click "Close Master" and watch the changes automatically take place across all slides.

You can change the font and size of tiles, the location of the title box, the bullet point type and much more. Anything you put on these slides can appear on every slide, such as your business logo in the bottom corner.

It is recommended not to have your logo on every slide. People watching your presentation will not forget the company you represent between the first and last slide. Start and end up leaving your company name on screen and maybe your name. That is enough.

Designing Powerful Slides

How should a slide look?

First let's take a look at some slides that don't hit the mark, then we will look at the elements of a good slide and how you should put it together. Below is a sample of three slides. See what messages stand out from these slides for you:

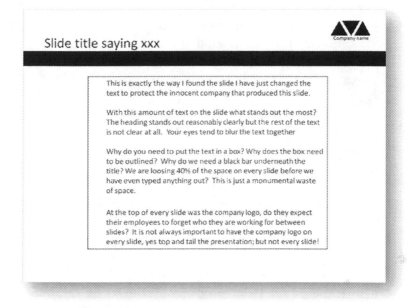

What stands out on this slide? Will your attendees be reading or listening to you? Why do you need a box round the text?

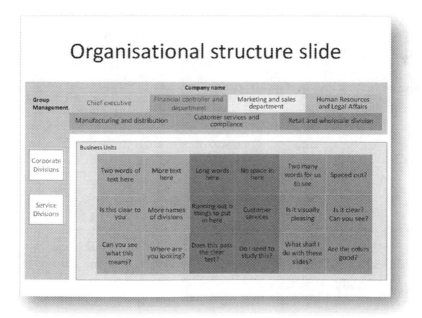

What stands out in this slide? Does the colour complement the slide? Can you tell what relates to what organisationally? Do you think there is a clearer way of showing this information?

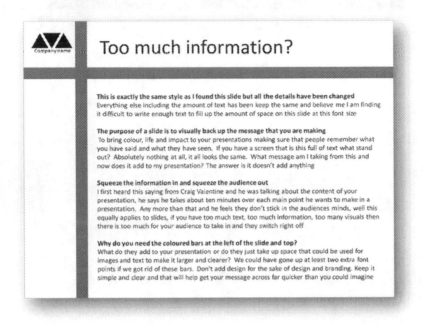

Do you think this slide will hold the audience's attention? What stands out on this slide? Do you think it is clear? How could you improve this slide?

These are real slides that people have used to try to enhance their presentations with just the text and names changed.

Text or Pictures?

Wherever possible, use pictures and only a few words. If using bullet points, keep it below a maximum of 6 followed by 3 or 4 words per line. This will make what is on screen stand out and be easy to read.

The slide should simply complement what you are saying, not say it for you.

There is a principle that will help guide you in the use of pictures on slides and it is the "rule of thirds". This rule is used by photographers when composing a picture. You will see that amateur photographers tend to place their subject right at the centre of the photograph. More seasoned photographers use the "rule of thirds" to place their subject off centre.

To take advantage of this rule split your slide into thirds horizontally and vertically as below.

In PowerPoint you don't have to imagine; PowerPoint will guide you. There are useful on-screen guides designed to help with the creation of slides. Simply right click on the main slide and select "Grid and Guides". This will present a dialogue box where several options will appear:

GRID AND GUIDES

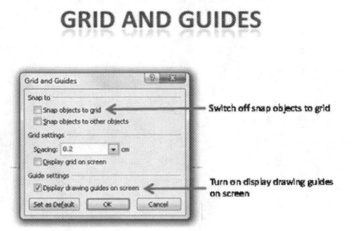

By selecting "Snap objects to grid", you will have greater control over the positioning of items on the slide. Switch on "Display drawing guides on screen" and this will enable you to easily use drawing guides to show the positioning on the slide in relation to the rule of thirds.

If you place guide lines at 3.25cm up and down on the horizontal axis and guides at 4.25cm left and right of centre on the horizontal axis you will be able to see the slide split into three by three.

The points where the eye is most drawn to on a slide are at the intersection of our guides. Place key items or messages along the lines and particularly at the intersections of the points:

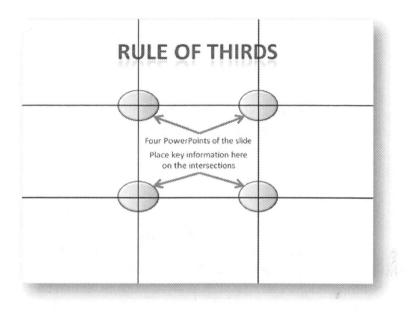

What do you think of the slide on the following page, which is designed with the rule of thirds in mind?

Is it clear what the slide is saying?

Would that back up the point you are trying to make?

When designing your slides, remember:

- Use images not text
- Keep bullet points to a maximum of 6 and three or four words per line
- Take advantage of the rule of thirds when designing slides
- The number of slides does not matter
- Slides should be clear, simple and quick to read

Attention & Animation

Should animation be used in slides? Does it detract from what you are doing? By animation, we mean controlling when parts of a slide are revealed to the audience bit by bit rather than all at once.

If used properly, animation can play an important role in your PowerPoint presentation. Good PowerPoint courses illustrate this point well by providing two demonstrations; with and without animation.

In the first demonstration, a slide containing an agenda appears on screen. The entire content of 6 or more bullet points comes into sight at once. In this scenario, the audience is likely to have missed what you were saying because they were reading whilst you were talking.

The most dangerous thing that happens when you put all your text up on a slide at once is that a delegate reads it and says mentally "I know this" because they will then switch off and not engage with what you are saying for the rest of the slide.

In the second demonstration, each agenda item appears using animation as it is discussed / presented. This enables complete control over what text the audience sees.. In this scenario, nobody reads ahead and misses what you are saying. Consequently, you will receive full attention and the text will reinforce each point as it appears without cause for distraction.

How should a standard slide be animated with bullet points?

It is extremely easy. Click inside the text box you wish to animate and then navigate to the "Animations" tab. Select the drop down box and the following options will appear:

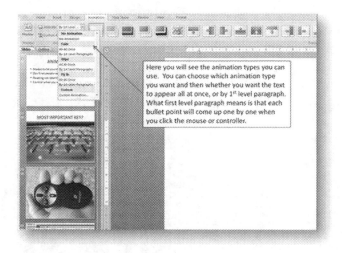

Experiment with each of the different animation styles to see which suits your presenting style.

Consider changing the order of items that will appear on the screen. This is far easier than it sounds. Let's say you have a slide with four items on it to appear. You want the items to come into sight in a certain order so that you can talk about them.

See the slide below:

Suppose you want the money and then property to fly in followed by the big sale and finally, the profit graph. To do this, you would need to use "Custom Animation".

Try opening the "Custom Animation" box that is on the "Animation" tab. The box will open up on the right hand side of the screen and look like this:

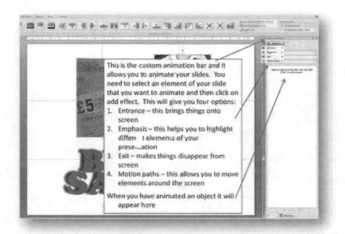

Highlight the four items and select an animation. These will appear in the right hand bar and the number on the animation will correspond to the number against the item on the slide. This shows the order of each animation. In our example, you can see from the numbers that the first item to appear will be the property followed by the money, then the big sale and finally the profit graph:

If you later wish to change the order of the animations, it is as simple as "dragging and dropping" the animations in the custom animation bar on the right hand side. You will instantly see the numbers on the right change as well as the corresponding number on the animated picture.

In summary, animation can be an important part of using PowerPoint. Remember these top tips about animating slides:

- Always have items pop up so your audience can't read ahead and then switch off whilst you finish talking
- Find an animation style that you like and be consistent with it throughout your slides
- If the order that things animate requires changing, use the "Custom Animation" bar
- Keep animations simple - complexity can detract from your presentation

Room Setup

Which side of the PowerPoint screen should you stand when presenting?

Try standing to the right of the PowerPoint slide or the audience's left of the slide. There is a simple reason for this. People read from left to right. You want people look at you and then their eyes will naturally go to the right to view the corresponding point and then their eyes automatically come back to you (the start) afterwards. This makes it easy for your audience to listen to you, look at the slide and then refocus on you.

The screen should also be slightly off to the audience's right hand side allowing you to be centre stage. The PowerPoint presentation is there to support you; not to take the lime light.

The following image is the ideal room set up for a PowerPoint presentation:

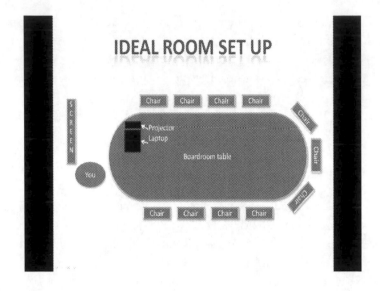

Your laptop should be in front of you so that you can see the current slide and the slide that is coming next. There should be no surprises when you click that remote.

Use "Presenter View". This shows the current and following slide. This way, you don't have to look at the screen behind. Just glance at the laptop in front.

To select "Presenter View", click "Slide Show" followed by Presenter View". You will need to have it set up on two screens to enable this as it provides a different view on your laptop to that which is displayed to the audience.

Typically (although this may differ for certain types of computer) to switch your PC to utilise two screens:

- Right click on the desktop and click "Personalise"
- Half way down the list should be a link to "Display Settings"
- When you have the projector plugged in, you will see there are two monitors in black numbered "one" and "two"
- Click on monitor two and select the check box for £extend my desktop onto this monitor"

When "Presenter View" is used, the presentation will be on screen two and your notes and slide view on screen one. It makes it really easy to see what is coming next and smoothes out the presentation – see the image on the next page.

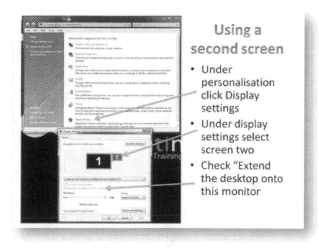

Using a second screen
- Under personalisation click Display settings
- Under display settings select screen two
- Check "Extend the desktop onto this monitor

Controlling PowerPoint

All good presenters use a remote control device to manage the flow of their slides. Without this valuable device, Every time you go to the laptop and turn away from the audience to change slides you lose rapport and connection

Invest in a good presenter's remote control with features such as:

- Left and right arrows to move slides back and forward and one animation at a time.
- A laser pointer to point to different parts of a slide.
- The most useful button of all is the square one at the bottom. This button does the same as pressing "b" on your keypad when you have a presentation up; it blacks out the screen. This is a button you need to learn to use more often, when you are telling stories, want the audience to focus completely on you or whilst an exercise is taking place.

You need to black out the screen so that it does not distract the audience.

If you are talking with the slide still in full view, there will be a handful of people within the audience be distracted whilst thinking about the font that has been used or where you got your pictures from or even something else. A blacked-out screen gives the audience no choice but to focus on you and what you are saying. PowerPoint should only be on display when you are directly referring to the slides.

What Do You Do If PowerPoint Fails?

Imagine the scene; you have been waiting to do you presentation for about an hour, there are 50 people in the audience, you start confidently, you flick the button to make the PowerPoint presentation appear and nothing happens….

The audience stares at you………..

You stare at the audience…………..

The projector has gone to sleep whilst you have been waiting and won't fire up in a hurry. What do you do? How do you overcome PowerPoint failing?

Don't say it won't happen to you. You need to be prepared. Here are some top tips for being prepared for a PowerPoint presentation failure:

1. Carry your presentation on a USB stick so that you can put it on someone else's laptop
2. Always have it saved in both 2007 and 2003 versions as people might not be able to read the version you have
3. Test the equipment before you arrive on site if you can, preferably the day before
4. If the video you are using shows on the laptop and not the projected screen, you need to select which will be the primary screen. Do this within the control panel, display settings
5. Double check cables for the projector and laptop the night before
6. Carry a VGA to DVI converter if using other people's machines

7. Take spare batteries for your remote control presenter
8. Carry slide handouts to use if all else fails

Conclusion

Becoming a top PowerPoint presenter doesn't happen overnight. Follow the steps in this guide and you will be well on your way.

Confidence comes from preparation and practice. Give yourself as much time as possible to perfect your presentation.

Here are some other things that you can do to increase the speed at which you become a great presenter:

1. Play with the software and create presentations for fun
2. Join a toastmasters club —a local one to you can be found by searching the internet
3. Watch other speakers and note down what you like and dislike, become a PowerPoint connoisseur
4. The Internet has a great source of speakers to watch. Hans Roslin provides an interesting view on how to present data
5. Join a PowerPoint workshop
6. There is no better way to improve than to get on stage and practice delivering your newly created slides
7. Most of all, have fun with it; if you enjoy giving your presentations then chances are, the audience will enjoy watching too

Your Checklist for Effective PowerPoint Presentations

MUST DO: Remember that PowerPoint is only a presentation tool. It is you that is presenting so ensure you have the attention of the audience with good eye contact, body language and engagement with the presentation in the background as a reference point.

To summarise, here are the top tips for using PowerPoint Stick to these and you will make an impression next time you use this great piece of software.

1. Write the presentation first then think if you need PowerPoint to help demonstrate it
2. Have a clear objective for your presentation that is easily measurable
3. Create a wire frame slide pack and organise it using "slide sorter" view
4. Use images wherever possible; not text
5. Use the rule of thirds to create visually stunning slides
6. Keep bullet points to a maximum of 6 with 3 or 4 words per line
7. Animate your slides to control what people see
8. Use a good remote control presenter
9. Use the key "b" to black out the slides when you want the audience's attention
10. Stand to the right of the screen so it is easy for the audience to read from left to right
11. Put the laptop in front of you so the slides come up as the audience sees them
12. Put the screen slightly off centre so that you are the centre of proceedings
13. Arrive early at the site and test the PowerPoint and projector facilities before people arrive
14. Write your presentation first then think if you need PowerPoint to help you demonstrate it.
15. Have a clear objective for your presentation that is easily measurable.
16. Create a wire frame slide pack and organise it using "slide sorter" view.
17. Use images where ever possible not text.
18. Use the rule of thirds to create visually stunning slides.
19. Keep bullet points to a maximum of 6 with 3 or 4 words per line.
20. Animate your slides to control what people see.
21. Use a presenter such as the Kensington Si600.
22. Use the key "b" to black out the slides when you want the audience's attention.
23. Stand to the right of the screen so it is easy for your audience to read from left to right.
24. Put the laptop in front of you so you can see the slides come up as the audience does.
25. Put the screen slightly off centre so that you are the centre.
26. Arrive early at the site and test the PowerPoint and projector before people arrive.

Step vii) The Recommendation

How to negotiate and successfully close a sale

You've gone a long way in getting toward the end of the sales process - now the final push.

We often feel awkward about trying to close a deal – perhaps we fear a rejection or don't want to appear pushy. What we really want is for the potential customer to say "Yes I like what you have and I want to buy it now, how much is it please?" Closing the deal is what this book is all about.

Without being able to effectively close a deal, the learning so far will do nothing for you.

In reality, the customer rarely gives you the contract without negotiation and final agreement to all the terms. Everyone wants to get a good deal or at the very least wants to avoid appearing too keen so that they end up paying more than they have to.

It's down to you to use your negotiation and closing techniques to secure the deal so that you can take the relationship to a contractual one where you get paid.

Objectives and Scope

In this section, we show you how to take your presentation skills and turn them in to a sales generating tool. Many people think presenting and selling are the same - they are not!

Presentations provide an opportunity to give information, to demonstrate the value of your service/product and to educate. To get that all important order, you will need to go through the final stages of the sales process; the recommendation, negotiation and close.

We will show you how to win business from your sales meeting, by developing your presentation to the final stage.

Having read this you will be able to:

- Make a relevant recommendation that will encourage the customer to buy
- Overcome objections and negotiate a win/win situation
- Use powerful closing techniques to get the business

Setting the Scene

Before you reach the stage of the recommendation and close, you will have had one or more meetings and discussions, within which you will have:

- Established rapport with the prospect
- Established their needs (Fact Find)
- Secured agreement that these are indeed their needs (consolidate the Fact Find)
- Presented your service/product

You are nearly there!

The next stage is to make a specific recommendation to the customer, based on your presentation and the prospect's needs.

Preparing Your Recommendation

At this point, you will have reached an understanding of how your product/service can meet the client's needs. Rarely though will this be just one simple answer. It's more likely that you can offer a range of solutions but you will need and want to start (in most cases) with a specific recommendation. This will then lead on to clarification and negotiation before you close the sale.

Once the recommendation is made, it's there in front of the customer so it pays to make sure that it is well thought through and that you have built in opportunities to negotiate.

One useful model is to think in terms of each element of your recommendation (e.g. price, specification, delivery) as being on a scale and the point you want to reach is an overall balance. As well as your specific recommendation on each element, there could also be areas where you can add value (and possibly up-sell) and at the other end will be your bottom line – the point at which you have no further room for negotiation. Filling in the following table (expand/change the elements as necessary) can help you to identify those parameters:

Item	Recommendation	Added Value?	Bottom Line
Specification			
Service level			
Delivery method			
Delivery/completion timing			
Price			
Funding/payment options			
Prestige (brand) value			
Your guarantee			

Some items might not be negotiable. Others might have either no bottom line or one set by factors outside of your control. This provides a very clear idea of what is being recommended and the areas where value can be added as well as your bottom line.

Making a Relevant Recommendation

Having made the presentation, aim to continue getting your customer's engagement and lead him/her to saying "yes" to your recommendation.

Here's the first key to getting that "Yes".

Start your recommendation by summarising the content within your presentation and its relevance to the Fact Find (their needs). Through everything you have done so far, this should be an automatic "yes" and keeps them in that habit.

> **Example:**
>
> **"So Mr Smith, you can see that our accounts service provides you with the flexible, low cost solution to managing your yearend accounts which was your main concern when we spoke earlier."**

Now pause to invite a response – it might be a nod of agreement - but assume you have got it right.

If the prospect makes a statement, or asks a question, deal with it and treat it as a buying signal.

If an objection is raised, deal with this with confidence (see later in the guide).

The key point is to make sure that you have addressed any potential objections before you get to the recommendation. For now, we'll assume you can move on and that you have dealt with any questions and objections.

You can then get to your recommendation. The nature of this will depend on the service or product you are providing, but it will include to two key elements:

- What you are offering them
- What you want in return

Most recommendations will include:

- From your position: A summary of your specification of delivery, term of agreement and the price
- From the prospect's position: This will address their needs, be in line with their time span and be within budget

It's possible that your customer will say "yes" at that stage and all you need to do is get them to sign on the dotted line. More often than not, there will be one or more points that they will want to amend. It might be the price, the delivery timescale – perhaps even the colour!

You are now entering into the stage of negotiations. You might look on this as having established their intention to buy; now it's about sorting out the final detail.

Your Price

People have different views on any price. Look at the many TV programmes there are where people try to guess the price of something – from houses to antiques. Whilst you might view these people as non-experts in the area where they are trying to guess the price (and your prospective customers are all clued up on the right prices, right?) it's still important to remember that rarely is price the issue – its value AND their budget.

Your aim should always be to demonstrate enough value before you reveal the price so that your prospect ends up thinking, if not actually saying aloud, "Gosh – I thought it would cost more than that."

This is NOT a failure of your pricing – unless:

- The prospect thinks it should cost twice as much! Somewhere between 25-50% is about right
- You can't make any profit at that price

We will deal with this tricky subject again later in the section below.

Step viii) Effective Negotiations

The purpose of negotiation is to come to an agreement that satisfies the needs of both parties. The aim of a win-win negotiation is to find a solution that is acceptable (or even better, desirable) to both parties and leaves all involved feeling that they've won – in some way – once the negotiation has finished.

In an ideal situation, you will find that the other person wants what you are prepared to trade and that you are prepared to give what the other person wants.

To help you negotiate, there are a number of things you can do which you should have done throughout the sales process. It is all down to communication. We have outlined these within this guide

They are:

i)   Show empathy and understanding with the prospect.
      You will be able to do this by listening to what you are being told and watching their body language (movement of eyes, head and hands give a big clue!)

ii)   Speaking convincingly
      Use an authoritative but friendly tone and make positive statements avoiding phrases like "I think will be able to help you....I believe our product is the best......"

iii) Show respect and understand the other person's values and beliefs

iv)   Be reliable and consistent in your messaging

Preparation

As always, this is key to success.

- List all the elements of your service that are essential to meet the client's needs - create the value. See the list below.
- Have some additional offers that you can afford to give as added value or as alternatives
- Assess your opening price and your bottom-line price

Here's a list of potential negotiation points other than price. You should know your bottom line for each element if applicable:

- Specification
- Service levels
- Delivery method
- Delivery/completion timing
- Ease of administration
- Funding/payment options
- Prestige (brand) value
- Your guarantee

Having thought through these elements, you are ready to control the negotiations by following these simple rules and tips.

Price and Negotiation

Every negotiation has its price. How many times have you heard?: "Drop your price by 20% and you've got a deal"

- "You will have to give me a retrospective rebate on volume if you want our business."
- "I'd love to do business with you but I don't have the budget"
- "I like all the services you are offering but we simply can't afford them. Could you include them at no additional cost?"

Every time you hear statements like these, you're in the middle of a potentially difficult sales negotiation. How you handle that negotiation will determine whether or not you close the sale and how profitable that sale will be.

Here's a crucial point to remember

"Negotiation isn't all about price"

If your buyer is in that 20% (the lower end of the market) where specification over a certain minimum counts for nothing. You get to know who these people are and in the long term you probably don't want to do business with them. They are treating your product/service as a commodity – i.e. they are all the same and all they want to do is buy from the cheapest source. Of course, if your product/service is a commodity, then you will know that this is exactly the market you are in.

The first thing to remember is that negotiation isn't all about price. You are trying to find a middle ground that satisfies both parties' needs. The more that you have made sure your proposition is full of value and reflects the needs of the prospect, the more likely you are to achieve a price/yield that is acceptable to you.

Think about the elements of your product/service that are important to the buyer. You could even try ranking them and get the customer to agree what is most important and what's less important. You then know what points you are more likely to be able to negotiate.

Don't Believe Everything You See and Hear!

When negotiating, you have to take everything you see and hear with a grain of salt. Buyers are good negotiators and thus they are good actors. You may be the only person who has what they need, but everything they do and say, from body language to the words they use, will be designed to lead you to believe that unless they get an extra 10% off, they are going with the competition. Be sceptical. Be suspicious. Test, probe, and see what happens.

Don't Offer Your Bottom Line Early in the Negotiation

The more desperate you appear the more you will give away. If you offer your bottom line too early, it won't be believed and the customer will probably try to push for a further reduction in price.

If you reach the bottom line, then say so and stick to it. If you move again after that, your bottom line is not believed and you'll lose even more.

Once the bottom line is reached, you are effectively saying "we either do this deal on these terms or I walk away." Make sure you are prepared to walk away.

Be Prepared To Offer Alternatives

Before getting to the bottom line, you should have explored other options, such as changing (lowering) the specification, altering the timing of delivery, etc. Make sure that you can still meet your customer's needs. If you can't meet a specific point, make sure they know. If you hide and then don't deliver on it, they will hold you to account.

Get Something in Return for Your Added Value

Your prospect may ask for an additional service that can be provided easily and at no extra cost. You may be tempted to say' "Oh, we can do that. That's no problem."

Before you do, think about your options.

- Throw it in as part of the package and try to build good will
- Without committing, tell the buyer it is possible. You may not be able to get him to pay extra for it but you may be able to use it as a bargaining chip in resisting price concessions

Sell and Negotiate Simultaneously

Think of selling and negotiating as partners. Sometimes one is to the fore and sometimes the other, but they are always both there. The buyer sees a salesperson demonstrating features, advantages and benefits. The hidden partner is that of a negotiator probing and seeking out information that may be valuable later when items such as price, terms, quality, delivery, etc. have to be negotiated.

Be Patient

Finally, it really is very important to be patient. Take your time, don't get anxious, stay calm and whatever you do, don't panic. Negotiation is something we all do from a very early age (there are no better negotiators than children!). As we get older, we sometimes don't practice those skills as much as we get used to compromise, etc. In these situations, you can use the negotiation process to your advantage if you practice. You'll be astonished at the difference that it makes!

Introduction to Overcoming Objections

We will go into this in more detail and give some useful skills and techniques to help you handle objections.

Initially it's important to remember that there are five basic objections that may be raised

- Belief in the product
- Relevance to the client
- Past problem
- Competition
- Cost

We mentioned earlier that you should restate the key benefits of your presentation and align them to your client's needs, in their mind. Having done this, during negotiations you should only encounter price objection!

However, if the prospect comes up with an objection, not based on price, this will often be due to one of two things:

- A need or opportunity has not been identified earlier within the Fact Find
- The prospect is "playing a game" and trying to gain an edge on negotiation

Either way, don't panic. You can maintain control.

Simply, show empathy and tell the prospect that you understand their point.

Then, use this as an opportunity to remind the client of the needs you both agreed earlier and why you have made the recommendation.

From here, maintain integrity, show assertiveness and get negotiations going again.

There is a useful acronym for the process used here, ERICA:

> **E**mpathise/agree with the customers point
> **R**efine to a specific area
> **I**solate
> **C**ommit
> **A**nswer and close

Here is an example of ERICA at work!

- Customer. I don't really think your service is what I want.
- You: I fully understand that you may have doubts in moving from your current provider. What in particular is worrying you?
- Customer. I need reliability of service from a larger organisation.
- You: Ok – apart from this is there anything else?
- Customer: No, I don't think so.
- You: That's fine - so you'd be happy to go ahead if we can sport this out?
- Customer: Well yes, if the price is OK

You ignore the price issue - leave that to negotiations.

- You: OK we can talk through price in a minute (deflect price discussion and leave to negotiations). You may remember from our discussion earlier that we give you a personal service because I am based locally. Perhaps I didn't mention that I have access to support from our national, well known company. They are there to answer any questions or concerns that you may have, which I can't immediately answer. Here are our credentials (present).
- Does that answer your concern?
- Customer: Yes

You have now established if you had missed something or if the client was playing a game, without alienating them. At this stage, by digging into the customer's objections, you are able to re-state the need and explore alternatives, add value, control your price reduction (if this is in line with your parameters) - ultimately leading to a win-win situation.

Win - Lose Negotiation

On occasions you may win business in a situation where you achieve your objectives but the buyer's needs haven't been fully addressed. This is a win-lose negotiation and should only be used if you don't need to have an ongoing relationship with the other party as, having lost in some way; they are unlikely to want to work with you again. Also beware of what they might then say to others you might want to do business with.

> **Example:**
>
> **They need something right now and you are the only one who can supply it but you are charging a premium price, knowing that they can't go elsewhere (on this occasion). You get a one-time sale but probably won't get repeat business.**

More about handing objections effectively

We touched upon objection handing earlier in the book.

Coping with objections will be key to your success. The meeting is in full swing, you've breathed a sigh of relief on a presentation well done. You have made your recommendation;- now you just want the business.

Let's get real! When you are involved in any type of sales activity, you will find that not everyone jumps at the opportunity to buy what you have on offer. This might sound obvious but it's amazing how many salespeople forget it and end up getting annoyed and frustrated with prospects that say "no".

Here we will look at why people say "no" what to do when they are not interested, they don't realise they should be a customer of yours and how you should handle the situation.

Objectives and scope

- To arm you with skills and techniques to be confident in dealing with objections
- To reveal the hidden need through the decision makers
- Identify the types of objection and how to overcome each one
- What to do when people really don't need or want your product

After reading this section, you will be able to:

- Identify the decision makers and know how to influence them
- Follow a 7-step process to handling objections
- Turn around indecisive prospects
- Maximise your chances of getting an order at the earliest possible opportunity

Objections

What Are They?

Firstly, let us be clear about what is an objection. An objection is a reason that a prospect puts for not proceeding at that point with the sale.

Any sale will involve reasons that are put up by your contact and some will hold more water than others. We need to understand the nature of that reason and then we need to find ways of dealing with it.

It is much better to reduce the chance of objections arising in the first place of course. Good questioning, research and customer intelligence will help. Ensuring you have good quality and a healthy number of relationships in the prospect company can also be critical.

Don't fall into the trap of only communicating with one person in your potential client's company, especially if you get on really well with them. We will talk more about the various types of people involved in a sale that can create or raise these objections later.

Real v False Objections

We need to recognise that not all things that people say should be taken literally or on face value. In a sales context, people say all sorts of things for all many reasons and frequently will back away from what they have said when you have been able to explore it further.

If you are selling prosthetic limbs and your client has a full complement of limbs, they can probably raise a large number of reasonable and unquestionable objections to buying your product.

If you are selling paper made in Scandinavia and the prospect says they can buy it cheaper from a contact in the Far East, then you can reasonably assume that this might be true and thus a "real" objection to your pricing.

However, the most common objection of "it's too expensive" can easily be raised when you know that you are within the prospect's budget and the product is appropriate. This is then a "false" objection.

False objections come in many forms but in essence they are all characterised by one factor: they do not stand up to scrutiny. Unfortunately, proving to the prospect that they are wrong is not always the best approach if it is a false objection. That is not to say you should not give them the accurate facts if they are actually misinformed. We are talking about the instances when prospects contrive a reason to not go ahead. Frankly, most people would much rather the prospect was honest, straightforward and direct about the reason for not proceeding or slowing the sale, but real life is not like that.

Why Do Prospects Raise False Objections?

They are not the right person to talk to

The major reason is because they have been caught out and they are not actually the main decision maker. We deal later with the Decision Making Unit.

Your response: learn to analyse whether the person to whom you are talking is the right person to pitch. If they are not, don't waste time handling an irrelevant objection. Work your way away from the monkeys and on to the right organ grinder.

There was never a need for the product

At one extreme, there are purchasing managers who need to keep busy and want to give the impression of needing your product. At the other end, they may have already decided on an internal source of supply but wanted to go out to the market to check pricing. Other times, it might just be a competitor checking you out.

Your response: put it down to experience and move on as quickly as possible. If you suspect that you have been consulted under false pretences, do your best to quiz your contacts and ultimately confront the reality with them.

The need for the product has gone

In long sales cycle products such as choosing auditing companies or non-essential training, the environment surrounding your product might have changed during the sales process. The prospect may give you a different reason for not proceeding but it amounts to the same thing! Often, the prospect may have been progressively slowing down the responses you may have required and may be a little embarrassed that they as a prospect have been the victim of circumstances.

Your response: keep in contact with the prospect. The need may well return but it may be months or years. As long as you don't make them feel bad about effectively wasting your time, you should be able to pick up where you left off. Don't be annoyed, your time was not totally wasted.

They may want to slow down the sale

Possibly things have moved forward at a pace with which they are not comfortable. They may be a personality profile that does not like to be rushed, even if all the ducks are in a row and they simply need to sign a purchase order.

Your response: don't try to force the pace, but don't give enough time for a competitor to come in.

They like you

Strange as this might sound, if you build a really good relationship with a prospect contact, they will feel guilty if they have had to choose someone else. Possibly someone above them has made a decision and they may still feel that you are the right company. But politically they may not reveal that maybe someone has pulled rank.

<u>Your response</u>: Leave the door open in case the prospect is let down by the alternative supplier. Your chance may yet come. Accept that possibly you were not speaking to the true decision maker anyway and that maybe you need to work further up the food chain when the need for your services arises again.

Incidental v Terminal Objections

Don't assume that you always have to satisfy every objection to take a sale forward. Sometimes you can deal with an objection by finding out if solving it will actually win the sale. This is always worth knowing. As with the distinction between false and real objections, you can divide objections into incidental and terminal. Then you know how much time and effort is required to put into solving it.

A terminal objection will result in something that can effectively lead you to closing the deal there and then, or it is the "deal breaker".

Example

You are selling vehicles to a fleet manager and their loads regularly exceed a certain weight. This is terminal. If your largest vehicle does not carry that weight then this sale is going nowhere. If they do, then you can carry on selling.

What is more, if the vans are up to capacity, you can turn this terminal objection into what is called a trial close or a pre-close. A bit like this:

"That is a good question. Just can I check – if our vans are able to carry that weight, would we have a deal?"

> **Example:**
>
> **As for the previous example but about satellite navigation. Now you can ask the same question: "If our vans did include it, would we have a deal?" If the answer is "yes", it might be worth considering throwing in free satnavs this time around to win the deal.**

Sometimes the objection is about something that is not usually included.

In the case of the satnav, if the vehicles absolutely MUST have it included, then it becomes a terminal objection. However, the prospect might say, "We don't have to have them but it is a bonus". Thus, whether they have satnav or not is incidental – you can still win the sale either way but it may become a negotiating point, by asking the question in the form we show here, we have revealed the importance of the objection.

The Decision Making Unit

One of the most common mistakes is trying to sell to the wrong person. This is why you need to be sure that you are pitching to the right people on one hand and finding them on the other.

There are different types of people in the sales process and we have looked at some of them in other guides. Different sizes of organisation will have varying numbers of people involved in a sale. Small organisations may only have one person who makes the decision. Large organisations will have a series of committees, stakeholders and purchasing processes.

The value of the sale will also determine the number of people that may be involved in the purchasing process. If you are selling paper clips then possibly one secretary in one department may be involved. If you are selling a multi-million pound resource planning system to an international company you may find dozens of people get a look-in.

Another factor is the formality of the buying process. Even in some large companies, significant sums can be spent at the whim of the Managing Director if they set up and run the company from the top-down. Some small businesses are run by a handful of people from the corporate world and they might apply cumbersome procedures before making the decision.

Don't make assumptions about how your prospect does their buying. You need to find out. The best way is to ask but often this won't be readily revealed. This is the time to do some detective work.

Thus we refer to a Decision Making Unit (DMU). This could be one person, it could be many. We will assume that you are selling to organisations that have several people in the DMU fulfilling different roles. If there is a single decision maker, then the understanding of the DMU is less relevant.

Let us first look at the possible component parts of a DMU and give some labels to typical people in it. Bear in mind that rarely will individuals fulfil only one DMU role and sometimes there may be multiple people in the same DMU role.

Ultimate Decision Makers

There will often be a single individual who takes the lion's share of the decision-making. Other people in the organisation will look to them to make a decision. Sometimes others will pretend that they have more of a say in the decision than they really do, and the ultimate decision maker will veto any decision if they want.

Ultimate decision makers can at one extreme be bullies that disregard the advice and input from other stakeholders in a purchase. At the other extreme they might be highly collaborative. You are better to assume they are highly collaborative and be wrong than the other way around. You do not want to upset or ignore other elements of the DMU because they may report this to the ultimate DM.

Specifiers

These are sometimes called "buyers" or "technical buyers" and their role is not so much to say "yes", but to say "no". They will logically and systematically analyse your offer against any brief. They are less likely to be interested in whether they like you or the relationship and are much more likely to be interested in warranty terms, costings and reliability.

Salespeople find specifiers amongst the most difficult people to deal with in a sale. The psychometrics or personality profile of salespeople is often the opposite of specifiers: people-orientated, creative, impulsive compared to the analytical, cynical and considered approach of specifiers.

Salespeople don't need to like specifiers but they do need to work with them. While sometimes it feels like specifiers are just getting in the way, they are performing a very important safety-valve and sanity check of any proposal.

As a rule, specifiers will seldom actively help you to get a sale, but they can easily stop the sales process. A large proportion of objections that arise in a sale are raised directly or indirectly by specifiers however, they are often easy to deal with: they will be factual and logical.

If your product or service is required to display a particular feature and it does not, you need to provide a reason to the specifier why it is not an issue or provide an alternative solution. Trying to make the issue seem smaller than it is will rarely satisfy the specifier.

Advocates

Sometimes referred to as "internal sponsors" or "coaches", advocates can be the oil in the machine of the sale. You will not always have the benefit of one but you will know when you have one.

Advocates want to see you win the sale. It could be because they recommended you to the DMU, you are friends, they owe you a favour or your solution in particular will be good for them in some way. If you find one, wine and dine them and don't be scared to get their guidance in the sale process.

Anti-Sponsor

We have all come across the situation where a competitor supplier has "someone on the inside" that is making your life difficult. This probably means your competition has an advocate. Their advocate is essentially working against you and is an anti-sponsor.

Anti-sponsors will help the prospect raise objections against your proposal. They might highlight your company's lack of experience against theirs or they might even provide inaccurate information about your suitability. It is likely to be obvious that an anti-sponsor exists because you seem to come up against blocks at every turn.

The temptation is to fight fire with fire. However, you cannot win that game because you are not party to the detailed discussions and politics within the client company. Focus on doing your best to show the product or service is best and maybe you need to keep closer and more regular contact with the prospect contacts.

The anti-sponsor may not have everyone's ear so work harder to find an advocate within your target company that can defend you from the inside.

Influencers

There are many stakeholders involved in major buying decisions. There are all manner of people that are affected if the company chooses the wrong product or service. Warehousing may wish to buy a new stock control system but Finance will want to be sure it interfaces well with their systems. Finance will not necessarily say "yes" or "no|" to your stock control system but their concerns may well infect your buying contact in Warehousing. So there is someone in finance that is an influencer.

In smaller organisations, the MD may want to buy 5 new mobile phones for the company but her husband may have a personal dislike towards the mobile phone network you represent.

The key is to engage influencers and to flush them out early. You can corner off any potential problems simply by asking the primary contact in the DMU who else is affected by their purchase, who has asked to be consulted or who has shown an interest in the purchase.

Influencers can plant the seeds of objections in your primary contact's head. You may suddenly get a non-technical person say that they just want to look into any potential clashes with other protocols in the company. Find out who put this idea into their head and try to communicate direct with this influencer.

Users

While a fleet manager may have the principal say-so in purchasing new vans for 20 engineers, the drivers themselves may become positive influencers and advocates if you can organise it. They will then apply pressure to the fleet manager – your principle buying contact – to go with you. Ignore the users at your peril and never lose sight of who will be engaging with your product or service.

Gatekeepers

This is a particular type of influencer – often a personal assistant or secretary – who has the specific job of keeping time wasters away from the decision maker, usually a senior director. Take every opportunity to be nice to gatekeepers be it engaging in friendly banter whenever you encounter them, all the way up to birthday presents when you get to know them better. All too often gatekeepers are around longer than their bosses and can hold the key to your winning the business.

Gatekeepers are often tasked with rejecting salespeople, usually at their first approach. It does not matter that your product or service could save the prospect company from disaster or save them millions of pounds. The gatekeeper is just doing their job and raising objections unthinkingly because they have been told to.

You can sometimes get gatekeepers on side by being one of the few people that actually treats them with respect and engages them. In that case, they can almost become an advocate, but that is rare.

Generally, you need to make it easier for the gatekeeper to help rather than to block you. Techniques include:

- Try to get sympathy: tell them that your boss is insistent you try to get a proposal out
- Keep calling and agree when you will call next. Eventually they might either take sympathy or respect your persistence
- Get them on side and ask for their help in getting to the decision maker

For more advice, refer back to the chapter "How to Get Past the Gatekeeper".

Decision Making Unit (DMU) Conclusion

Essentially you need to consider who you are talking to and pitch accordingly. If you are speaking to an influencer or gatekeeper, don't sell them on the benefits of your product; rather try to find a way through to the real decision makers.

If you are speaking to a real decision maker then always be employing detective work to uncover the other elements of the DMU.

Don't rely on one decision-making contact in an organisation. You might be doing brilliantly with one contact but they might move departments, their deputy might take over or they might leave the company. You are then back at square one and need to deal with a whole set of new objections. If you have cultivated other contacts that were aware of the positive approach of your previous contact you have a much better chance of maintaining continuity.

The Seven-Step Process

We have a standard 7-step process that can work as a checklist whenever a prospect raises an objection. This might be an objection to setting an appointment, receiving a proposal or in the final close of a sale. The process works the same. This is built around the principle of **E.R.I.C.A** which we covered earlier

1. Listen

This might seem obvious but it is amazing how often salespeople make assumptions, especially if they speak to numerous prospects each day. By listening properly, they can avoid the mistakes others might make.

Also, real listening makes the prospect feel valued and believe you are sincere. Since so much of selling is about building rapport and relationships ("people buy from people they like") this is critical to giving you the best chance of convincing the prospect that you will truly solve their objection.

Listening is an art and a virtue displayed by the best salespeople. They don't just *hear*, they *listen*. Listening is active, hearing is passive. In fact, "active listening" is recognised being listening where we do something to prove to the listener (and ourselves) that we really are processing what is being said.

Examples of active listening include:

- Nodding
- Repeating back what has been said in a different form
- Obvious note-taking
- Noises of acknowledgement such as "uh-huh", saying "indeed", "I see", "please go on" etc.
- Asking relevant questions to explore the point being made

> **For example:**
>
> **"If we can't do it in green, are you saying that you will not buy from us?"**
>
> **The prospect may respond to the affirmative, and you now know if you can proceed with the sale.**
>
> **They might say:**
>
> **"Actually, to be honest, it is not critical because it won't be seen most of the time".**

2.   Check

This is closely aligned to active listening but is not just done for effect. We really do need to make sure our understanding of the objection is the same as the prospect's. This stage also allows us to gauge how important the objection really is.

Now you will have an idea how much time, effort and cost you might need to invest in solving the objection.

3.   Isolate

Have you ever had the merry-go-round sale where every time you answer the client's objection and you ask them for their credit card details they say:

"Oh, and there is another thing, do you have it in large?"

And this happens several times? Of course you have.

This gives more control to the prospect as they dictate to you when the close comes, plus it takes longer to complete the sales process.

Would it not be better to have all the objections out on the table in one go? Then you can prioritise them and see if there is a deal breaker, in which case you need not worry about the "incidental objections".

The phrase "apart from…" allows us to more quickly expose all the objections in one go.

> **For example:**
>
> **"Apart from your concerns about the size, are there any other issues we need to box off before I can arrange delivery?"**

It is important to remember not to just say this once, reveal an objection, and then ask for the order. We keep saying it until the prospect eventually says: "No, I think that is it".

We may have 10 objections but we do have them all out in the open now!

4.   Probe

We should have a comprehensive list of objections raised by the prospect. Now we want to understand more about each of them. For example:

- How important is this issue: is it a deal-breaker?
- What exactly needs to happen for it to be solved?
- Do we need to find out more information in order to resolve the objection?

This is achieved by asking questions about each of the objections. Importantly, this stage is still about information gathering and we do this for each objection in turn. We don't yet solve the objections.

5.   Answer

When all the information needed about objections is obtained, only now do we attempt to answer them in turn. In many cases you may need to go away and find out more information.

If you don't feel that you can answer ALL the objections in one sitting, don't start. If you have a list of objections, this gives you an opportunity to make sure you have the right answers to all of them and maybe even find out connected issues that will arise nearer to the fulfilment of the product or service.

You should agree a time and place to deliver the answers to all the objections in one go. Avoid the temptation of answering most and coming back with the answer on one later. This could allow your competition an opportunity or allow the prospect to more easily play you against another supplier.

6.   Confirm

Immediately after answering each objection in turn, include a quick confirmation. Again, don't assume you are answering their objections. This makes you seem all the more collaborative and a caring, conscientious supplier plus reduces the chance of mistakes.

Simply ask: "So does this address that particular issue, before I go on?"

If the answer is not "yes", go back to the Probing stage.

7. Close

We won't deal with closing here. In fact, if the previous 6 have gone well, you won't have to do an awful lot. If you have answered all the objections, there is only one obvious conclusion for the prospect. They would be mad not to buy from you!

Questioning Skills

Consider yourself a detective or a doctor. It is your job to find out as much about the person in front of you as possible so that you can make the best assessment. To do this, you need to ask powerful questions. We have dealt before with questioning skills and shown in the 7-step objection handling process how important this is.

In general, you want the prospect to talk unencumbered. The best tools for this are "Open" questions. These are questions that are difficult to answer "yes" or "no" such as those beginning with the words:

- When...?
- Where...?
- Who...?
- How...?
- Why...?
- What...?

These sorts of questions invite the other person to talk freely.

Conversely, "Closed" questions are much easier to answer "yes" or "no" and these often start with:

- If...
- Did...
- Can...
- Was...
- Do...
- Are...

These questions are often used for assertiveness to more easily control a conversation.

Assertiveness

This is not to be confused with being pushy. Assertiveness is about having self-worth and not allowing yourself to be bullied. When the customer is coming up with objections, they may often make them sound like accusations or criticisms of you, the product or service but this is rarely the case. Even if it is, so what?

Sometimes you need to take the situation by the scruff of the neck and stop talking around the situation. If the client is doing something wrong, failing to understand a point or not allowing you to respond to their objection, you need to know how to stand up for the cause. We don't have the space here to talk about assertiveness but successful objection handling is as much about how you say it as what you say. Again, you need to be assertive and take control.

Logic v Emotion

It is often said that customers make their real decisions based on emotion and then justify them immediately with logic. It often sounds like people are buying the red sports car for logical reasons such as speed of getting to meetings, good resale values, etc!

People buy from people they like. They usually like people for emotional not logical reasons. So build the relationship with the members of the DMU. There will be issues and there will be objections raised to your proposal at some point.

You are more likely to get a chance to deal with these if you already have a good relationship with your contacts that goes beyond the mere transaction. Make a point of getting good at small talk. This will help you to maintain a positive relationship when it comes to the difficult times of handling the objections.

Motivation

It is easy to take so many objections from a prospect that the wind is knocked out of you or you just lose the desire to win the business. If the facts have not changed – you still know the prospect needs what you are offering – don't give up unless it is absolutely necessary to do so.

Remember why you wanted the piece of business in the first place and remind yourself how good your product is. There are plenty of techniques to keep up your motivation in the face of a barrage of objections be they music, exercise or visualisation. Remember your dreams and goals or sheer bloody-mindedness!

If It Is Obvious They Have No Requirement

Get out. Don't waste their time and say that you don't want to. More importantly, don't waste your time.

Before you get out, make sure you leverage their time.

- Ask them for referrals. If they are a nice person they will feel a certain guilt and obligation that you have made the effort to visit, so ask them if they know someone who might be a good prospect. Don't be shy to push for an actual introduction
- Be certain that there is no potential need in the future. If there might be, then get a timescale
- Can you get referrals for contacts of yours? This might seem bizarre but you can generate goodwill and return referrals if you find out that they need a good solicitor and you happen to know one. It's a long-shot, but if you don't ask, you don't get!

When They Say "Yes"

Remember that you are going to the meeting in order to win the business. On rare occasions, the appointee will make a purchasing decision at the meeting.

Be optimistic and be prepared for this. If you need order forms, take them with you to the meeting and fill them in there and then and get the signature.

Alternatively, a sales or purchase order may be required. Make the call to the relevant departments if necessary and get this pinned down there and then if you can.

Conclusion

You should now be better equipped to handle objections that you will inevitably get in a sales role. Learn to analyse the nature of an objection so that you know which technique or tool you need in order to deal with it. Also, know when to work around an objection because there may not be a sale to be made there.

Persistence is the key – don't take no for an answer too easily. Don't badger but do be methodical and you will win some of those sales that your competitors leave on the table.

Your checklist to handing objections

> **MUST DO:** Dont take a prospects initial objection as being a barrier to success. When faced with an objection always keep asking 'is there anything else concerning you?' until you have isolated all their *real* concerns. Remember –it is all about E.R.I.C.A

Empathise/agree with the customers point
Refine to a specific area
Isolate
Commit
Answer and close

Identify the type of objection

Incidental/terminal

Identify the decision maker(s) and the decision making process

Employ the 7-step process:

- Listen
- Check
- Isolate
- Probe
- Answer

- Confirm
- Close

If no, can you get referrals and then get out

If yes, confirm details

Section ix) Powerful closes to get the order

There are numerous theories and techniques on how to close a deal.

For the owner of a smaller business, keeping the close as simple as possible is often the best way. Sophisticated tricks can come across as aggressive or pompous, so why use them?

Here are some simple, powerful closes.

Sharp Angle Close

Make a major statement followed by a minor question:

"It's been great to hear that you can really see the value of our service and that it's within budget. When do you want to start?"

The Direct Close

You've done all you can to find a win-win situation so ask for the order and stop talking! This is also known as the silent close.

The Alternative Close

We have mentioned options a few times within this guide. Offering alternatives can make a powerful close, as they lead away from a yes/no situation. Make sure that you can deliver two or more solutions and then ask, "Which do you prefer?" This changes the dynamic slightly as instead of asking for a yes/now you are leading towards a conclusion that they are creating through your alternatives.

Can You Avoid The Close?

If you have secured agreement to the customer's needs and shown how your recommendation delivers the solution and they have agreed, you might think the close is not needed. This can happen where your approach is perceived more as a consultation than sales meeting. Just remember that it is important for the customer to realise that the next action (could be the next meeting) is one that involves money.

Can't Get Them To Agree To The Close?

If so, they still perceive a risk to the deal. Your job is to take away the risk so that you get customer satisfaction (delight).

- Is your guarantee good enough – have you taken out the risk?
- Can you offer a free trial period?
- First xyz is free
- Demonstrate reliability

For example, it is unlikely somebody would buy a car without test driving it first.

As part of your preparation to the close, have you got answers to all the obvious (and some not so obvious) questions the customer might ask about your product/service? If you haven't, it should not come as a surprise if you can't close. Customers need to feel totally confident that you have thought it through from their point of view and can fully deliver.

Confirm the sale in the client's mind

Great. You have won the business. To make sure the customer understands fully what has happened and feels in control, here are a few tips:

- Inform the customer what will happen next
- Ensure they have your full contact details
- Ensure all documentation is complete and that they have signed the order if appropriate

- Explain future levels and methods of contact
- ...and most importantly, thank them!

What to Do When You Lose the Sale

Even at the end of all that presenting, recommending and negotiating, you might reach the situation where you and the potential customer can't agree on a deal. What do you do?

Here are some alternatives:

- Walk away – there's no point in doing a deal that doesn't deliver what you need out of it. Move on to the next opportunity.
- If there really is no prospect of you doing business with them in the future, consider "selling" the lead to a competitor who you think will be able to help them. You might at least earn a commission or referral fee.

What if you've lost out to a competitor? Think in terms of "losing it for now, not forever":

- Find out why you lost – if you really have built up a good relationship with the prospective customer, they shouldn't mind sharing this with you.
- Then, subject to any changes you might need to make your product/service better fit their needs in the future, offer to be the alternative supplier if it doesn't work out with the competitor. Make them feel that they can still come to you, without any feeling of embarrassment.
- Make a diary note to follow up in whatever period of time is suitable – may be a week, month or 6 months.

Sometimes, the potential customer will pick another supplier even though you "know" you made the best offer compared to the competition. If this is the case, you need to stay in the loop as they should find out, sooner or later, that yours was the offer they should have gone for. Always make it easy for them to come back to you; no-one likes eating humble pie!

Conclusion

Closing the deal is the last step of the sales process. By following the process through, getting the order will have been an easier and more pleasant experience than without a structure. It should also be more profitable.

The close will have been made on the basis of building rapport, identifying and agreeing the client's needs, presenting your offering specifically aimed at addressing their needs. The recommendation and close form a logical end to the process by achieving a win/win situation for all concerned. Enjoy it!

Checklist to closing the deal

Prepare Your Recommendation

Item	Recommendation	Added Value?	Bottom Line
Specification			
Service level			
Delivery method			
Delivery/completion timing			
Price			
Funding/payment options			
Prestige (brand) value			
Your guarantee			

Recommend

Stage 1 – Summarise your presentation and relate it to the customer's needs. Seek agreement to this.

Stage 2 – Deal with questions and objections.

Stage 3 – Make your recommendation, addressing needs, specification, timescale, budget, etc.

Negotiation

Know your bottom line – refer to your preparation.

Find out what elements are the most important to your customer and identify areas where you can/cannot negotiate.

Remember:

- Negotiation isn't all about price
- Don't believe everything you see and hear!
- Don't offer your bottom line early in the negotiation
- Be prepared to offer alternatives
- Get something in return for your added value
- Sell and negotiate simultaneously
- Be patient

Close the sale using the appropriate method and make sure that both the customer and you have exactly the same understanding of what has been agreed.

Consolidate the sale – confirm the details in writing

Chapter Four

How to deliver great customer service and generate more sales

Well done-you've won the business, you can relax now can't you?

Well, not really. Successful businesses leverage further revenue opportunities from their customers by providing good service and satisfying their further needs.

Understanding the level of service your clients would expect from you is a vital first step to developing the service level required to maintain and increase the number of clients using your services.

Your customers will already have high expectations of the service level they should receive before they engage you. Meeting, or preferably exceeding, that expectation will mean you will retain and gain more clients **and ultimately, charge more!**

Finally, isn't it more satisfying servicing clients you know and like compared to prospecting for new business? Don't miss the opportunity!

Objective and Scope

This chapter provides a full understanding of what clients think about customer service and how to operate and provide exceptional service. We also show how easy it is to deliver, at no extra cost, exceptional service and how to maximise a return on this investment

After reading this, you will be able to:

- Understand what makes great service and how to put together a process to deliver it

- Maximise the opportunities that come from having good customer relations
- Maintain good and effective customer contact after developing the relationship; and
- What is the difference between bad, indifferent, good and exceptional customer service

What Constitutes Bad, Indifferent, Good and Exceptional Customer Service?

Interesting question! When you walk into a restaurant and are greeted by the Front of Restaurant staff in a warm friendly way with a smile, does that constitute good or exceptional customer service? If no one even looks at you and you're left standing there until either you walk up to him or her or walk out, does that constitute bad or just indifferent service?

The difference is not just down to the level of service you provide but also your customer's expectation of the service they feel they should receive! When you walk into a cafe or a burger place, you expect a certain level of service; when you walk into a top London restaurant, you would be horrified to receive the same level of service as the cafe! It's all down to managing and exceeding expectations. Conversely, you might feel very uncomfortable receiving the top London restaurant level of service when walking into a café or a burger place.

A story for you to reflect upon! Here's the key to it.

BU lives in **B**ad customer service **U**niverse, IU lives in **I**ndifferent customer service **U**niverse, GU lives in **G**ood customer service **U**niverse and EU lives in **E**xceptional customer service **U**niverse.

There were four customers, each living in parallel universes. They were called **BU**, **IU**, **GU** and **EU**. They all booked the restaurant over the Internet to celebrate 18 years of marriage. It was to be a romantic meal for two and they were really looking forward to it!

BU arrives at the restaurant to find it doesn't have the booking and, to add insult to injury, it doesn't really seem to care either! After enquiring what the restaurant intends to do about it, BU is told "well, it's not our fault, there's nothing we can do, we're fully booked and anyway you should have phoned to get confirmation." BU protests, "The website confirmed the booking." The Restaurant replies, "You can't trust that, we don't control it, it's not our fault!" After further protestation BU is given a table and has a meal. BU complains and is ignored but pays £120 for the meal and leaves very unhappy and disappointed. BU promises never to return and to tell everyone possible how bad the restaurant was.

IU has better luck. He arrives at the restaurant to find they have the booking and is greeted in a matter-of-fact way. IU is about to go through to the table when the restaurant says that the table is not ready yet but will be shortly. Fifteen minutes, and many apologies, later IU is taken to the table however, he is politely reminded that patrons sitting at the table must wear a tie. In IU's universe the website did not say a tie was needed so he had to borrow one from the restaurant, which was very embarrassing. IU pays £120 for the meal and leaves thinking that could have gone better. IU did not complain but vowed to find an alternative restaurant in the future and never return.

GU had received a confirmatory email from the restaurant with the time, date and reference number of the booking. GU arrives and is greeted by a friendly person with a smile and is taken to the table straight away. GU if offered drinks on the house at the end of the meal, which are accepted. GU feels the £120 bill for the meal was 'a bit steep' but the meal was good and the evening pleasant.

EU booked the restaurant via the Internet just like BU, IU and GU. The website in EU's universe allowed for other things to be communicated to the restaurant at the time of booking. EU was able to put in that they were celebrating their 18th wedding anniversary that night, where they were coming from, the registration number of the car and any special requests. EU knew there was a lovely view from table three so had requested that table. EU's confirmatory email showed the time, date, booking reference, a map of how to get to the restaurant, where to park and how long it would take to drive from their postcode to the restaurant and a link to the menu and wine list in case they needed to pre-order any of the dishes. The email also contained the dress code. EU later received a text message with the booking reference, so there was no need to record that separately to take with them.

When EU parked the car, they were met by a member of staff from the restaurant who introduced himself as John and welcomed them by name. John explained which path to take to get to the front door of the restaurant. When EU arrived at the door, it was opened by another member of staff who said "EU, my name is Jane, welcome and thank you very much for choosing us to celebrate your 18th wedding anniversary." John had called Jane to let her know that EU had arrived and was about to come into the restaurant; John got this information from the registration number of EU's car!

Peter arrived (Jane had spoken to Peter before EU had arrived at the door) and introduced himself; "Hello EU, I'm Peter, thank you for choosing our establishment to celebrate your 18th wedding anniversary, please follow me to escort you to your table." EU followed Peter to table three where there was a hand-written **post-it note** on the vase congratulating them on 18 years of marriage and wishing them a pleasant evening.

At the end of an exceptional meal, EU is presented with a bill for £240 and doesn't even blink because EU is very happy to pay it as the evening has been wonderful, EU feels like a highly valued client and has been made to feel as if nothing is too much trouble.

Eleven months later, EU received an email from the restaurant asking if he would like to book a table to celebrate his 19th wedding anniversary!

Taking yourself and your staff through the experience your customers will have when buying your services, you are able to see what level of service you offer and where improvements can be made to move it from bad or indifferent or good to exceptional. Once you've identified and altered those areas that need improving, and provide the level of customer service experienced by EU, you can charge more even though it doesn't cost more to produce!

Where Does the Process of Customer Service Start?

A number of organisations believe customer service starts when a potential client either phones the organisation or walks into reception. This is not the case! The customer's "experience" of your organisation starts the first time they come into contact with you or what/who represents you. You can move ahead of the competition by ensuring that your website is firmly client focused. Is your website easy to navigate or is it impossible to find basic information about what you offer or how to communicate with your organisation? Is it set up for the benefit of the IT department for when it needs to make changes or for your clients who might want to get in touch or just have a quick look at the latest position on a particular point? Give away some intellectual property on your website; tease your clients to come to you for more or in depth advice; that is when you can charge them.

Can your customers gain some benefit from you just by looking at your website? If you don't have full contact details, direct to the fee earners, then you are putting barriers in the way of your (and potential) customers from getting in touch; the competition that does not do this will take your customers away from you!

When your staff meet people at networking events, do they receive exceptional customer service? Now, I hear some people saying "receive exceptional client service at a networking event; what is he talking about?" Yes, how you and your staff interact with potential and existing customers will give an indication of your views on the level of service your organisation offers. Do you reflect the organisation well at networking events? How you behave at networking events is how the organisation will be viewed! Training your staff on how to be successful at networking can make an incredible difference to your business.

Price v Service: The Percentages

In studies carried out by respected organisations, it has been shown that:

- Only 9% of people will leave an organisation because of price. If you put up your hourly rates tomorrow - **creating pure profit because you're not increasing the cost of producing the work** - you would lose only 9% of your customers. It is very likely that part of the 9% will be those who always quibble over the bill (getting you to reduce each one) and taking up more of your time arguing about the bill or asking for "free" advice.

- A further **68%** will leave because of "indifferent" customer service; that's not bad service, rather, **'indifferent'** customer service. Imagine your practice retaining that 68%, or a large portion of it. What would that do to your database to which you can sell more of your services? What would that do to the marketing budget required to win new clients and replace those leaving? What would that do to the amount of extra revenue you could produce from those existing customers?

Just like EU, most people do not mind paying more if they feel they are getting **value for the service**.

Creating Ambassadors for Your Business

Providing exceptional service to your **external customers** will ensure they become your ambassadors. The same can be said for providing exceptional service to your **internal customers** will ensure they become your ambassadors.

Your staff are your internal customers and reflect your organisation externally. The way your internal customers are treated will be reflected in the way they treat your external customers.

If you provide your staff with a comfortable, pleasant and efficient working environment and one where:

- The equipment helps produce more rather than hinders them
- They feel they are part of the team
- They feel that if they offer suggestions or make proposals those are considered – seriously – and implemented if appropriate
- They see those who own the business leading
- They feel the firm values their input
- They are praised publicly and criticised in private
- They feel their contribution is recognised
- They are rewarded correctly – and not just in terms of finance, and
- They are respected; then,

They will provide exceptional service to your external customers.

Your mission is to make your external customers to be your Ambassadors. The more they talk in a positive way about you and your organisation, the more likely you are to gain more customers. Taking a very happy client to a networking event who will then tell others there how great your business is and how happy they are is a much better use of money than placing an advert in a local directory stating what you do. Demonstrate rather than declare. Testimonials are a very good thing to have. Imagine having a testimonial that states "this is the fourth time I've asked the business to work for me and will be doing so again!"

To achieve this, you need to be providing an EU customer service.

Maximise the Opportunities from Giving Great Customer Service

The objective of giving great service is clearly to generate more business. However customer service alone won't achieve this.

Here are some useful tips:

i)   **Constantly "sell" to them – the "post-it note" touches that mean so much!**

Let's go back to our earlier story. GU experienced good service but those **post-it note** touches EU experienced distinguished EU's and GU's universes. The restaurant had considered the following beforehand:

- EU did not have to worry about the dress code
- EU did not have to "hope" to get table three
- EU's party did not have to announce themselves at the door
- John, Jane and Peter knew, and used, EU's name to make him feel more important
- EU experienced those **post-it note** touches, The Restaurant had thought about how to make EU feel even more valued

The correct level of service you offer will move you from GU's to EU's universe and into a higher charging range! Here are some simple ideas that can have a powerful and positive impact:

- Send your client an email confirming the meeting and give details of directions and parking facilities
- Ensure that your receptionist and secretary know who is visiting so they can give them a warm, personal welcome, by name upon arrival.

There are many ways of adding little touches to the service you provide, all of which are available now, that will elevate you to EU's universe.

Simple attention to detail like recording how a client likes their tea can make a positive impression when you meet next time, Once confirmed he would like a drink, your secretary says to him, "It's milk with one sweetener, isn't it?" to which he is likely to reply, "That's impressive and yes, thank you."

ii) Are you set up for you or your customer?

A number of organisations seem to be set up for their own benefit rather than for the customer. In a service business, it is essential that you are accessible to your customers when they want to get hold of you. Closing at lunchtime is not being customer focused because many of them won't be able to get away from work other than in their lunch hour. Turning the phones off at 5pm and not on again before 9am means you is not easily accessible.

There are two ways of dealing with this:

- Ensure the phones are answered outside of normal office hours – within reason – so your customers can access your service at their convenience. Of course, there need to be parameters set around this so your staff are not answering the phone 24 hours a day!

- Ensure voicemail messages and emails are replied to within one working day. This might seem a bit obvious to many of you but this does demonstrate good customer service.

Consider whether your business is set up for the benefit of those working in it or for your customers.

iii) Know what the customer wants

How do you know what your customer wants? Finding out through good communication at the beginning, during and after the relationship enables you to be constantly aware of what they want and expect to receive from you.

At the beginning, communication is established between you, always ensuring full awareness of the times when it will be difficult to get hold of your customer, when is it easiest for them, not you. What do they prefer, phone, mobile, email, letter? There is a great line from a film that fits perfectly here – "Assumption my dear is the mother of all screw ups!" Never assume what you offer is what your customer wants. Don't ever presume the customer will be happy with what you offer. Find out what they want and then charge accordingly.

If they want snail-mail, give them just that and charge more because it costs you more to produce. If they want an answer to a question within 30 minutes every time, set up your system to guarantee this and ensure they get it but charge them more. They will pay it because they want value more than price. Any customer who wants price over value is not worth having!

Case Study

A potential customer has asked for a quote for some work that must be completed within four working days. Your reply should be that this could be done but other work would have to be put to one side therefore, there would be a higher charge than normal. In this scenario, the opportunity materialises into a signed-up customer who will be happy to pay the extra amount because of the perceived value received from you placing them in priority over other work.

In our earlier example, EU was happy to pay £120 more for the same meal as BU, IU and GU because of the value EU received.

iv) Explain what you expect from the customer

Part of providing exceptional customer service is to establish a "contract" of responsibilities.

To provide an EU type service, you need to let your clients know what is expected of them, so that you can deliver your side of the contract! Some might say that that is a bold statement. Well, it's not!

Progressing a service agreement for someone requires as much communication from him or her as it does from you. If you need answers to questions and don't receive them, then you can't get on with your work and provide EU's customer service experience. Telling your customer precisely what they need to do in order for you to maintain an exceptional level of service is vital.

For example. Customers paying your invoices at an agreed time helps provide exceptional service. Constantly worrying about the bank balance and chasing customer who don't pay their bills will distract you from concentrating on the work ahead.

v) **Ask your customers what method of communication they want to use**

Consider this. A law firm refused to communicate with any of its clients by email because…; well, really it was because the partners were frightened of email so instead of learning how to use it and how it could save them money and time, they simply refused to listen to their clients who were requesting communication by email.

If your customers want to use snail mail, why force them to use email? As it costs you more to send out letters, charge more to use this method, tell them you're going to charge more and why.

By maintaining an open dialogue with your customers about what they want, you will know how to interact with them. If you don't, you may well be forcing them to go to your competitors though your ignorance.

How Do You Maintain A Customer, After Developing The Initial Relationship?

This is probably one of the areas where many businesses fall down. Maintaining a relationship with your customers is very easy if a system is put in place to maintain regular communication with them.

Including customers in your newsletters publications is essential. Sending out an email newsletter, again giving away some intellectual property, which keeps their interest, is a great way of keeping yourself and your company in their mind. You want to ensure you are uppermost in their mind the next time they need the kind of services you offer.

The newsletters should not be simply trying to sell them something. They should be genuine in their content. What can you give away to whet the appetite? What can you talk about that they would be interested in to maintain contact? What will bring them back to you each time?

Inviting a customer, (even if you are not actually doing something for them at the time) to networking events is a great way to maintain contact. You can sell it to them on the basis that they could pick up a new contact, client or piece of work from others they meet. It is a business development potential.

Dropping a customer the occasional hand-written note about something they would be interested in or at their birthday means a great deal. It is impossible to do this if you don't "know" your customer.

Case Study

A law firm wishes to gain greater profit and exposure from its existing clients posted a "new home" card to arrive ahead of completion to all their residential conveyancing clients with a hand-written note inside from the fee earner and secretary. They also sent out a checklist, about one month before completion to remind the clients of all those small but important things they needed to do and when they should be done that could be so easily overlooked; e.g. cancelling the milk and newspaper delivery,, buying "new home" cards, what to do a week, the day before and on the actual day of completion.

Maintaining a system of recording information about your customers enables you to stay in contact so you are always in their mind.

We would advocate all professional services organisations use social media to stay in contact with their clients, and then send out messages on a regular, and in a very cost effective way to maintain contact. These messages should not be simply pushing out your sales or marketing information but a way of giving away some intellectual property that will **benefit** your customers.

When your marketing team is creating these messages, ensure they firstly ask themselves "What **benefit** will our clients derive from reading this?" If they don't have the answer, don't send the message!

Social media is an incredible and powerful tool that can be fully exploited to retain and gain customers in the most cost effective way.

At the end of each transaction with a customer, ask them what they thought of your service and how it could be improved, through a short questionnaire; this is another great way of staying in contact. Use open ended questions to get bad, good or very good comments. If you use a scale, always use an even number of options. If you use an odd number of options you leave your client with the ability to "sit on the fence".

Here are some tips:

i) **Constantly 'sell' to them – the 'post-it note' touches that mean so much!**

Let's go back to the story I told you earlier. GU experienced good service. But those **post-it note** touches EU experienced distinguished EU's and GU's universes.

- EU did not have to worry about the dress code, The Restaurant had thought about that beforehand.
- EU did not have to 'hope' to get table three, The Restaurant had thought about that beforehand.
- EU's party did not have to announce themselves at the door, The Restaurant had thought about that beforehand.
- John, Jane and Peter knew, and used, EU's name to make him feel more important, The Restaurant had thought about it beforehand.
- EU experienced those **post-it note** touches, The Restaurant had thought about how to make EU feel even more valued, beforehand.

The correct level of service you offer will move you from GU's universe to EU's universe and into a higher charging range! Here are some ideas:

- Send your client an email confirming the meeting and give details of directions and parking facilities.
- Ensure that your receptionist and secretary know who is visiting, so they can give them a warm, personal welcome, by name.

There are many ways of adding little touches to the service you provide, all of which are available now, that will elevate you to EU's universe.

Very simply, I once recorded how a client liked their tea and when I saw him the next time and he confirmed he would like a drink, my secretary said to him, "It's milk with one sweetener, isn't it?" to which he said, "That's impressive and yes, thank you."

ii) Are you set up for you or your client?

A number of organisations seem to be set up for their own benefit rather than for the clients. In a service business, it is essential that you are accessible to your clients when 'they' want to get hold of you. Closing at lunchtime is not being client focused because many of your clients won't be able to get away from work other than in their lunch hour. Turning the phones off at 5pm and not on again before 9am means some of your clients will not be able to ring you easily.

There are two ways of dealing with this:

- Ensure the phones are answered outside of normal office hours – within reason – so your clients can access your service at their convenience. Of course, there needs to be parameters set around this so your staffs are not answering the phone 24 hours a day!
- Ensure voicemail messages and emails are replied to within one working day. This might seem a bit obvious to many of you but I know one professional services practice that, even in 2010 still opens at 9am, closes at 1pm, opens again at 2pm and closes at 5pm. There is no email, voicemail facility or mobile number; there is no website or even a fax line. Everything has to be put in writing!!!

Is this practice set up for the benefit of those working in it or for their clients?

iii) Know what your client wants

How do you know what your client wants? Finding out through good communication at the beginning of the relationship, throughout the relationship and after the initial relationship is over means you are constantly aware of what your clients expects, wants and receives from you.

At the beginning you establish the communication between you, you ensure you are aware of the times when it will be difficult to get hold of your client, when is it easiest for 'them', not you. What do they prefer, phone, mobile, email, letter? There is a great line from a film that fits perfectly here – 'Assumption my dear is the mother of all screw ups!' Never assume what you offer is what your client wants. Don't ever presume the client will be 'happy' with what you offer. Find out what they want and then charge accordingly.

If they want snail-mail, give them snail-mail and charge more because it costs you more to produce. If they want an answer to a question within 30 minutes every time, set up your system to guarantee this and ensure they get it but charge them more. They will pay it because they want value more than price. Any client who wants price over value is not worth having!

I work with one professional services firm who said to me that a potential client had asked for a quote for some work but the work needed to be completed within four working days. My reply – tell the potential client this could be done but other work would have to be put to one side so there would be a higher charge than normal – the potential client became a client and was very happy to pay the extra because of the value he received from the firm in dropping other work for him. EU was happy to pay £120 more for the same meal as BU, IU and GU because of the value EU received.

v) Explain what you expect from the client

Part of providing exceptional client service is to establish a 'contract' of responsibilities.

To provide an EU type service, you need to let your clients know what you expect of them, so that you can deliver your side of the contract! Some might say that that is a bold statement. Well, it's not!

Progressing a service agreement for someone requires as much communication from him or her as it does from you. If you need answers to questions and don't receive them, then you can't get on with your work and provide EU's client service experience. Telling your clients what they need to do in order for you to maintain an exceptional level of service is vital to then providing that level of service.

For example, your clients paying your invoices, at the agreed time, helps you to provide exceptional service – constantly worrying about the bank balance and chasing clients who don't pay their bills does not assist you to concentrate on the work in front of you.

v)   **Ask your clients what method of communication they want to use**

I worked with one law firm who refused to communicate with any clients by email because...; well, really it was because the partners were frightened of email so instead of learning how to use it and how it could save them money and time, they simply refused to listen to their clients who were requesting communication by email. Conversely if your clients want to use snail mail, why force them to use email. As it costs you more to send out letters, charge more to use this method, tell them you're going to charge more and why?

If you communicate with your clients about what they want, you will know how to interact with them. If you don't you may well be forcing them to go to your competitors though your ignorance.

Conclusion

Who is client service about? Well, the clue is in the sentence but is something organisations often forget! It is about the client!

If you had to use your organisation, how would you feel? How would The Restaurant staff in BU's universe feel if they were treated the way they treated BU? Would they feel valued, important? Would they feel The

Restaurant cared that they were a client or cared that they returned? Would they become an ambassador for The Restaurant, telling others how good it was? How would they feel in EU's universe?

> **MUST DO:** 'Walk through your own client journey' is a bit of a cliché now; however, experiencing what your clients experience is a great way of establishing what kind of service you offer. You might think what you offer is good or exceptional so be bold and ask those who experience it and then change your service according to what you hear. Aim for the EU Universe!

Checklist to delivering great customer service

- ☐ Review you customer service approach. Is their experience?
  - ☐ BU
  - ☐ IU
  - ☐ GU
  - ☐ EU

- ☐ Identify where clients first experience your organisation.
  - ☐ What is their experience?
  - ☐ Is your website client focused?
  - ☐ Is your networking client focused?

- ☐ What do you need to do to create internal ambassadors?
- ☐ What 'post-it' note touches can you add to improve client experience?
- ☐ Do you know what your clients want?
- ☐ What is each one's preferred form of communication and can you deliver that?
- ☐ Does the client know what you expect from them?

Summary

Within this book, chapter by chapter we have gone through the 10 stages of the sales process and along the way given you some confidence building tips.

As we said at the outset, the purpose of this guide was to give you a tool-kit for making a good sale and keeping that new client satisfied.

It is a frame work to work to, but don't forget that selling is as much about personality as it is about process.

You now have the ability to control the sale; just maintain your sense of humour and endearing qualities. This is important because you won't always succeed in getting a sale but by taking control of the process and maintaining a sense of proportion, you will still feel like you are a winner.

In the preface to this book we mentioned some **MUST DO's** which, even if you do nothing else, will make your sales calls more effective. Here they are again.

MUST DO: Know what benefits your company delivers and practice delivering this in under 45 seconds. This will form the basis of effective networking and starting your sales calls

MUST DO: Networking

i)   Make sure you have prepared youself well mentally and physically. Just before you enter the room, check in the mirror, remind yourself of a great thing you have done recently and enter the room chest out, shoulders back, exuding confidence!

ii) Before moving on from a discussion, swap business cards and ask to engage on LinkedIn-send an invite soon afterwards.

MUST DO: Always enter details from business cards and other sources (e.g. emails received) and put them in a simple spreadsheet to start with, All your client records must be in one place

MUST DO: Have your powerful introduction including your benefit statement written down. This will help you in engaging with the gate keeper and decision maker.

MUST DO: In the meeting listen more than you talk by asking relevant questions. Be yourself and don't panic-rejection isn't personal and someone will say 'Yes'

MUST DO: Remember that PowerPoint is only a presentation tool. It is you that is presenting so ensure you have the attention of the audience with good eye contact, body language and engagement with the presentation in the background as a reference point.

MUST DO: Dont take a prospects initial objection as being a barrier to success. When faced with an objection always keep asking 'is there anything else concerning you?' until you have isolated all their *real* concerns. Remember—it is all about **E.R.I.C.A** (**E**mpaphise, **R**efine, **I**solate, **C**ommit, **A**nswer)

MUST DO: Walk through your own client journey Experience what your clients experience and review your proposition on a regular basis

Now it's time for you to put all the knowledge you have gained into practice. Don't worry about making mistakes, just learn from them, move on and remember that rejection isn't personal.

Enjoy the experience and remember-people buy from people -so be yourself.

Mike
Mike White

www.cansellwillsell.com